Rowan
Fraser
6.00

D0469659

Lester Sumrall

THE DARK HOLE OF

WORLD HUNGER

And The Christian Solution

Unless otherwise indicated, Scripture quotations are from the King James version of the Bible.

Scripture references marked NKJ are taken from the New King James Version of the Bible, copyright 1979, 1980, 1982 by Thomas Nelson, Inc., Nashville, Tennessee. Used by permission.

Scripture references marked TLB are taken from The Living Bible, copright 1971 by Tyndale House Publishers, Wheaton, IL. Used by permission.

Scripture references marked NIV are from The Holy Bible: New International Version, copyright 1973, 1978, 1984 by the International Bible Society. Used by permission of Zondervan Publishers.

Scripture references marked NAS are from the New American Standard Bible, copyright The Lockman Foundation 1960, 1962, 1963, 1968, 1971, 1972, 1973, 1975, 1977. Used by permission.

Scripture references marked AMP are from The Amplified Bible, copyright 1965 by The Lockman Foundation. Used by permission of Zondervan Publishing House.

THE DARK HOLE OF WORLD HUNGER
AND THE CHRISTIAN SOLUTION

Copyright © 1989 by LeSEA Publishing Company
South Bend, IN 46624

ISBN 0-937580-23-6

Printed in the United States of America. All rights reserved under international Copyright Law. Contents and/or cover may not be reproduced in whole or in part in any form without the express written consent of the publisher.

TABLE OF CONTENTS

BOOKS BY DR. LESTER SUMRALL

- Adventuring With Christ
- My Story To His Glory
- Take It—It's Yours
- Gifts & Ministries Of The Holy Spirit
- Alien Entities
- Battle Of The Ages
- Beyond Anger And Pity
- Conscience—The Scales Of Eternal Justice
- Demons The Answer Book
- Bitten By Devils
- Ecstasy—Finding Joy In Living
- Faith To Change The World
- Faith Under Siege; The Life of Abraham
- Faith-Filled Words (Frank Sumrall)
- Fishers Of Men
- Gates Of Hell
- Genesis—Crucible Of The Universe
- Hostility
- Hypnotism—Divine Or Demonic
- Imagination—Hidden Force Of Human Potential
- I Predict 2000 A.D.
- Jerusalem, Where Empires Die—
        Will America Die At Jerusalem?
- Jihad—The Holy War
- Living Free
- Making Life Count
- Miracles Don't Just Happen
- 101 Questions & Answers On Demon Power
- Paul—Man Of The Millennia
- Run With The Vision
- Secrets Of Answered Prayer
- Sixty Things God Said About Sex
- Supernatural Principalities & Powers
- 20 Years Of "I Predict"
- The Mystery Of Immortality
- The Making Of A Champion
- The Names Of God
- The Promises Of God
- The Reality Of Angels
- The Stigma Of Calvary
- The Total Man
- The Will—The Potent Force Of The Universe
- The Human Body
- The Human Soul
- The Human Spirit
- Trajectory Of Faith—Joseph
- Three Habitations Of Devils
- Unprovoked Murder
- Victory And Dominion Over Fear
- World Hunger
- You Can Conquer GRIEF Before It Conquers You

Dedication

This book is dedicated to the *youth* of all nations.

The *youth* of the *giving* nations.

The *youth* of the *receiving* nations.

I wish to salute you.

I love you!

The younger generation is the hope of tomorrow on this planet.

Introduction

I have visited and spoken in over a hundred nations and on all continents, in more than fifty-five years of ministry. I go where hunger causes terrible suffering and deprives innocent humans of life. I do not go to take dreadful pictures of malnourished babies near death from hunger or sickness, but to personally feed hungry people, and to minister in Jesus' name. Then I return to challenge you, not to gasp in horror, but to rise up and help me feed the people and especially those who pray "Our Father who art in heaven...give us this day our daily bread."

Only you can answer the prayers of those good people caught up in the devastation wrought by civil war, famine, drought and the other contributing causes of world hunger.

I go where world hunger is at its worst today—places such as Costa Rica, Jamaica, Bangladesh, Nicaragua, Mozambique, Zimbabwe and Poland on the Czechoslovakian border.

It has been a learning time. The pace I keep would be difficult for most men many years younger than I am. At age seventy-six I should perhaps think of retiring, but the

Lord has renewed me as in the days of my youth. I am filled with energy and health to carry out the work that God has called me to do. The plight of God's hurting people and the cry of those who have not yet heard the Good News drives me forward to keep on running with the vision.

My mission is to inspire God's people to help fulfill the vision the Lord gave me in Jerusalem, that of feeding the world's hungry and being obediently responsive to the Word of God.

1 The Curse of Hunger

Sin brings consequences. Among other things, Adam and Eve's disobedience brought curses to the ground. The book of Revelation reveals that someday there shall be "no more curse" (Revelation 22:3).

The devil gets blamed for a lot of things, some of which may not be of his doing. Don't misunderstand, if you know me at all, you know I am an enemy of the devil. But sometimes people tend to pitchfork everything off onto the devil and refuse to take any responsibility for their own actions. One thing for sure I can tell you the devil has had a hand in, and the problem is food.

The Subtlety of Satan

The big blunder with Adam and Eve began in the Garden of Eden, and it began with food. Satan, in the form of a speaking serpent, beguiled Eve, and he did it through food.

He 's been using food ever since as a means of tormenting the human race. Food was the first temptation, and have you ever stopped to think that it was food that Satan used to try and tempt Jesus? (See Matthew 4:13; Luke 4:14.)

Hunger does terrible things to people. The gnawing sensations that initially accompany hunger pangs give way to frightening and unspeakable actions; but later, when hunger's victims are so weakened they cannot stand, they no longer cry out. Their strength is so gone they can't even make sounds.

Certainly one of Satan's most devious strategies against mankind is in this area of food deprivation.

Eve wasn't hungry when the serpent outwitted her. The devil must have laughed with hellish glee when Eve succumbed to his trick. Eve was vulnerable and foolish. Satan struck a fatal blow and the whole world is still reeling from its dreadful impact.

Adam had two voices pulling him in two different directions. God's charge to him not to eat from the tree of knowledge pulled him one way, while the voice of his wife pulled in another direction. Adam made a choice and we today live with the ultimate tragic results.

Our present-day difficulties and suffering situations worldwide are the results of man's sinful choices. Because of what Adam sowed, the earth has not always produced as God intended. Because of the transgression of our first parents, natural disasters have come upon the earth that have wrecked havoc with the soil and food production. Adam was told, "Because you have listened and given heed to the voice of your wife, and have eaten of the tree of which I commanded you, saying, You shall not eat of it, the ground is under a curse because of you. . ."(Genesis 3:17 AMP).

Sin brings consequences. Among other things, Adam and Eve's disobedience brought curses to the ground. The book of Revelation reveals that someday there shall be "no more curse" (Revelation 22:3).

Meanwhile, the awful curse of hunger stalks the earth grimly reaping what was sown so long ago.

Through the long centuries, many Christian, humanitarian, and government organizations have sought ways to alleviate the hunger problem in the world. You will read about the history of hunger in this book, some of the causes, and what has been and is being done for earth's suffering poor and needy.

While I have long been involved in intense world evangelism and ministering to orphan children in other lands, in more recent years God arrested my attention about the plight of the world's hungry while in Jerusalem, and presented to me one of the greatest challenges of my life. The End-Time Joseph Program to Feed the Hungry is the result. Prior to this, I had two life-changing visions that directed the course of my life. Now, in my latter years, this new vision has created a fire within me that is sending me around the world ministering in Jesus' name, strengthening and nourishing physically and spiritually God's hungry people.

The First Vision

In Panama City, Florida, when I was seventeen years of age, I saw my first vision. On one side of my bed was a coffin and on the other side a Bible.

Though I was in the last stages of tuberculosis, God said He would heal me if I would preach.

To this challenge I answered positively and began my ministry.

The Second Vision

Eighteen months later at a country school house near Dyersburg, Tennessee, I saw my second vision. I vividly saw heathen nations go to hell. I became so concerned that I wept all night and God said He was calling me to those nations.

The Missionary

Eighteen months later I was on a boat in San Francisco Harbor going to the mission fields of the world. Since then, I have gone to over a hundred nations on planet earth to preach the Gospel.

The Fifty Years

This has now been over fifty years. When I would ask God why I did not see another vision, He said that the visions of my youth were to send me forth as an evangelist and later a missionary.

The Third Vision

In more recent years, while in Panama City, Florida, I was sitting on the front row of a church and, as I closed my eyes in meditation, I saw a River of Blood. It was as dramatic as the two other visions that I had seen.

I told the church and pastor about it that evening.

The following night in Birmingham, Alabama, as I was praying in church during the song service, I again saw in a strong manner this River of Blood. I thought it could mean judgment and so I told the people to pray, and to write the date on the flyleaf of their Bibles.

The Tree of Life

A few days later I was in Denver, Colorado and a pastor said that the Lord had given him a prophecy concerning me.

He said my life was like a planted tree and that there were many branches on the tree.

He saw a limb representing the missionary churches I have raised up. He saw a branch representing the more than a hundred different books and syllabi I have written.

He saw the television stations as a limb on the tree.

He saw the Christian Center Cathedral of Praise in South Bend, Indiana as a strong branch.

Then he looked at me and said, "Now a new branch will grow on your tree of life. It will be a large limb and more productive, with more satisfaction than any other branch on your tree of life."

"The End-Time Joseph Program" In Jerusalem the New "Branch"

I was leading a tour group in Jerusalem in November, 1987. One night I suddenly woke up at ten minutes to midnight, after going to bed at eleven p.m.

God said, "It is also midnight in prophetic time. Listen to Me.

"One of My greatest concerns is that My people, part of My church, do not suffer death by starvation before I return. Will you help feed them?

"To them it would be an angelic food supply! It would be a miracle!

"I say to you, hunger is an agonizing death. Give to those who are dying and you shall live happily and victoriously.

"I speak to you in Jerusalem. It is the city where I took the bread and blessed it and said, 'Take eat, this is My body broken for you.' So take bread for the spirit, soul and body to the multitudes of the earth.

"Go especially to famine and war areas where there is devastation and hunger and feed them.

"Many are suffering. You will bring the food in fast by plane. You are to ride with the plane, watch the food being given out, and rejoice to see the children fed.

"Give food to refugees who require help. It is My pity upon them.

"America has the food. Buy it and take it to the hungry.

"Use storage houses to hold the food until you are ready to distribute it to the hungry."

The Lord said, "If I bless you financially for your needs, will you operate a global feeding program for My people?

"You will distribute the food through pastors and churches. Around the world I want you to feed My people who are hungry.

"Don't let My people die of starvation."

My response at nearly five a.m., after listening to God for five hours, was: "I am willing Lord."

The Lord said, "Then you will understand, the River of Blood flowing toward you is life flowing deep and wide. At times the blessing will be almost uncontrollable. Get ready for it!"

2 A Look at Biblical Famine

Famine: A state of extreme hunger suffered by the population of a region as a result of the failure of the accustomed food supply.

Mass starvation is not new in world history. The Bible is not silent about famines that decimated the population and neither are the history books and world literature. Most recorded famines have resulted from widespread crop failures caused by frost with prolonged winters, hail and cold summers; by droughts, followed by dust storms and loss of seeds; by crop diseases and plagues of locusts, pests or rodents; by the ravages of war and civil disturbances with the devastation of rural regions during periods of upheaval; and by natural disasters such as floods and earthquakes.

Other less direct factors may contribute to famine. The breakdown of food distribution systems may affect regions dependent upon importation of food. Deforestation may increase the danger of floods with subsequent loss of fertile top soil. Overpopulation in many parts of the world reduces the acreage per farm until it is barely sufficient to afford miserable sustenance in good years, with no ability to store any surplus for lean seasons.

In more recent years the plight of the poor has surfaced in countries where large multinational corporations have been pushing the poor off their meager land holdings, robbing them of their only means of raising food to feed their families. Many of these are government-sanctioned monopolies who are developing a tremendous power base at the expense of the people who are left to starve. There are people starving in the shadow of these industries who have sapped these countries.

Except in tropical regions, the peril of famine has always been great in primitive societies because of crude methods of food production and the absence of adequate methods of storage.

Man-made Plagues

There is another aspect of famine that is recorded in the pages of history and that we, in our generation, have heard about, but it is one that we can hardly fathom. It is man's inhumanity to man; it is the fate that befalls innocent people when wicked rulers use famine to break down the resistance of those whom they perceive to be their enemy. In more recent years, we have watched in horror as the television screen portrays in all-too-vivid detail the suffering of thousands wandering homeless, clothed in rags, their meager belongings on their heads, or sitting in their poverty, pitiful figures of despair.

We have reacted with unbelief as we hear of the famine in Sudan, caused by government action, with warring rebels using food as a weapon against the suffering millions caught in the middle. National magazines portray the eyes of hunger and the trail of bones—human bones, the remains of those who collapsed along the trails fleeing for their lives—while cynical rulers and rebels starve the people to improve their bargaining positions. We find this untenable. . .how, in civilized society, can this happen? But the unthinkable has happened and is happening.

Early Civilizations and Famine

Early civilizations were subject to famine. The first reference to famine can be found in the Old Testament when Abram left Canaan and "went down to Egypt" (Genesis 12:10). Famines were not uncommon in ancient Palestine. Genesis 26:1 tells us "Now there was a famine in the land—besides the earlier famine of Abraham's time. . ." But this time the Lord told Isaac not to go down to Egypt, but to stay put and He would bless him.

Actually, Egypt in the Scriptures is pictured as a symbol or type of the world, an instance of dependence upon some human source apart from God (see Isaiah 31:1). As Christians, we "go to Egypt," spiritually speaking, when we depend upon something or someone else for guidance instead of God.

Abraham's sojourn in Egypt was marked by problems. He had to resort to deception, he thought, and pawned his wife off as his sister (see Genesis 20). The thing displeased God and angered the king. The account turns out alright, but it afforded Abraham, his family, and his servants a good bit of frustration, danger and embarrassment. Sin evokes a price and always effects others. Perhaps Isaac was familiar with the story of what happened to Abraham and so the warning from the Lord was heeded.

A famine that "was over all the face of the earth" (Genesis 41:56) that is perhaps one of the better known famines, occurred at the time Joseph was made a ruler of Egypt. The Bible tells us this famine "ravaged the land" and was "very severe" (Genesis 41:30).

Joseph prophesied of this famine to Pharaoh as he interpreted Pharaoh's dreams and told him what to do to prepare for this. He described the famine in words that fit what we in our lifetime have seen happen in various places throughout the world. Famine this "woefully severe," Joseph said, leaves people destitute in their starving condition, and it exhausts, consumes and finishes the land (Genesis 41:30).

Actually, it was Joseph's provision that saved the people much suffering. It was Joseph's wisdom that provided a means of escape from death by starvation. And it is the biblical account of Joseph that God used to call my attention to the need to prepare now for the years of suffering and famine that are ahead.

There was a famine in the days of Ruth. Displacement of whole families often occurs at the time of famine, and that's what happened to Elimelech and his wife Naomi from

Bethlehem who made their way to Moab. Their sons married Moabite women. When Naomi's sons and her husband died, Naomi determined to return to Judah because she had heard that the Lord had "visited His people in giving them bread" (Ruth 1:6).

Famine as Divine Chastening

That famine occurs as a result of divine chastening cannot be denied. Famine occurred in David's time and he clearly recognized it was God's hand of judgment (2 Samuel 21:1; 1 Chronicles 21:9-13).

So great was the suffering by famine that the Bible tells us in desperation the people were reduced to cannibalism, that is they ate their own sons and daughters. This was prophesied in Deuteronomy 28:53 and fulfilled in 2 Kings 6. It is a terrible story, but faithfully recorded for our learning:

> And a great famine came to Samaria. They [Syria] besieged it, until a donkey's head was sold for eighty shekels of silver, and the fourth of a kab of dove's dung [a wild vegetable] for five shekels of silver. As the king of Israel was passing by upon the wall, a woman cried to him, Help, my lord, O king!
>
> And the king said to her, What ails you? She answered, This woman said to me, Give me your son, so we may eat him today, and we will eat my son tomorrow.
>
> So we boiled my son, and ate him. The next day I said to her, Give your son, that we may eat him, but she had hidden her son.
>
> — vv. 25-26, 28-29 AMP

The siege and distress was so great that even gentle, sensitive and refined men became so desperate, and so lacking in compassion they became cruel and desperate, and grudging towards their wives, sons and daughters, and resorted to eating them. Likewise, delicate, tender, well-bred women ate the afterbirth following the delivery of children, and then ate the children themselves secretly.

> You shall eat the fruit of your own body, the flesh of your sons and your daughters whom the LORD your God has given you, in the siege and desperate straits in which your enemy shall distress you.

> The man among you who is sensitive and very refined will be hostile toward his brother, toward the wife of his bosom, and toward the rest of his children whom he leaves behind, so that he will not give any of them the flesh of his children whom he will eat, because he has nothing left in the siege and desperate straits in which your enemy shall distress you at all your gates.

> The tender and delicate woman among you, who would not venture to set the sole of her foot on the ground because of her delicateness and sensitivity, will refuse to the husband of her bosom, and to her son and her daughter, her placenta which comes out from between her feet, and her children whom she bears; for she will eat them secretly for lack of all things in the siege and desperate straits in which your enemy shall distress you at all your gates.

> — Deuteronomy 28:53-57 NKJ

By the Sword and Famine

The psalmists and the prophets spoke often of the sword and famine as coming upon the people because of their departure from seeking after the Lord. In particular, the prophet Jeremiah cried out to the people, pleading with them and warning them of impending suffering if they would not forsake their evil ways (see Jeremiah 42).

Then hear now the word of the LORD, O remnant of Judah! Thus says the LORD of hosts, the God of Israel: "If you wholly set your faces to enter Egypt, and go to sojourn there, then it shall be that the sword which you feared shall overtake you there in the land of Egypt; the famine of which you were afraid shall follow close after you there in the land of Egypt; and there you shall die."

— vv. 15-16 NKJ

They were told not to go into Egypt, but they would not heed the word of the Lord coming to them by the prophet and they died by the sword and famine (Jeremiah 44:12-29).

"The Fever of Famine"

Jeremiah's prophecies were fulfilled with the siege of Jerusalem, January 587 B.C. until July 586 B.C.

The book of Lamentations describes in horrific detail this siege of Jerusalem and the defeat of the people. We see once again the pitiful fate of children who are always the most vulnerable when destruction and famine hit.

How the finest gold has lost its luster!

For the inlaid temple walls are scattered in the streets! The cream of our youth—the finest of the gold—are treated as earthenware pots. Even the jackals feed their young, but not my people, Israel. They are like cruel desert ostriches, heedless of their babies' cries. The children's tongues stick to the roofs of their mouths for thirst, for there is not a drop of water left. Babies cry for bread but no one can give them any.

Those who used to eat fastidiously are begging in the streets for anything at all. Those brought up in palaces now scratch in garbage pits for food. For the sin of my people is greater than that of Sodom, where utter disaster struck in a moment without the hand of man.

Our princes were lean and tanned, the finest specimens of men; but now their faces are as black as soot. No one can recognize them. Their skin sticks to their bones; it is dry and hard and withered. Those killed by the sword are far better off than those who die of slow starvation. Tenderhearted women have cooked and eaten their own children; thus they survived the siege.

— Lamentation 4:1-10 TLB

The Execution of Judgment

The prophets Amos and Ezekiel continue the dirge, with Ezekiel even acting out his prophetic words in some very dramatic ways. It was all to no avail. God, speaking through the prophet, told them in plain words that "the terrible arrows of famine [would be] for their destruction" (Ezekiel 5:16) so that they would know He is the Lord.

No More Reproach of Famine Among the Nations

But the God who executes judgment, is a merciful God when His people repent and turn from their wicked ways. Such is the message that Ezekiel is called upon to give as he foretells of the rebirth of the nation of Israel and God's new covenant with them.

God's Name cannot be profaned without a price being paid. He is a holy God. "Therefore I poured out My fury on them. . ." the Lord explains through the prophet Ezekiel. "I had concern for My holy name, which the house of Israel had profaned among the nations wherever they went" (Ezekiel 36:18a-21 NKJ).

The promise of restoration brought with it the assurance that He would bring no more famine upon this nation. "I will multiply the fruit of your trees and the increase of your

24

fields, so that you need never again bear the reproach of famine among the nations" (vs. 30 NKJ).

Jesus Spoke of Famine

The accounts of those years of suffering and famine undoubtedly filtered down from survivors to their later offspring. So when Jesus came along ministering to the human needs He encountered, when He spoke He made mention of the three and a half year drought that swept across the land and the famine that resulted during the time of Elijah the prophet (Luke 4:25). The effect was one of astonishment upon the hearers (vs. 32).

We know that Jesus was very conscious of the physical hunger needs of the people. Two of His most amazing miracles had to do with feeding the multitude (the feeding of five thousand men in addition to the women and children with five loaves and two small fish as told in John 6:5-14 and Mark 6:35-44; and the feeding of four thousand with seven loaves and a few fish as told in Mark 8:1-9).

Jesus warned that there would be famines, pestilences, wars, earthquakes and terrible natural disasters at the end of the age and preceding His second coming (see Matt. 24; Mark 13; Luke 21:5-38).

Through all of biblical history, it is easy to trace the hand of God correcting the oppression of the poor, allowing catastrophes, national destruction, captivity, natural disasters, and suffering at the hands of merciless rulers upon people who rebel against Him.

The call to us at this pivotal point in history is to learn the lessons from the past, and to determine with God's help to be the kind of people He wants us to be.

3 The Black Horse of Famine: A History of World Hunger

Famine: Extreme and protracted shortage of food, causing widespread and persistent hunger, emaciation of the affected population, and a substantial increase in the death rate.

The black horse of famine has been riding across the pages of human history unidentified by the vast majority of the world's people. Few there are, even among many Christians, who recognize the reality of the Four Horsemen of the Apocalypse: Pestilence, War, Famine, and Death described by John writing from the isle of Patmos (see Revelation 6:5-8).

"Sow the wind and reap the whirlwind," the prophet Hosea exclaimed. "The standing grain has no heads; It yields no grain" (Hosea 8:7 NAS). This is famine, the result of God's good plan for the earth and its people opposed

26

by rebellious sons and daughters of the earth. Man's sin—sin against God, against his fellow man, and against the environment—bringing separation from God with the whole creation now groaning in agony. SIN. Just a little three-letter word. But it presents a picture not understood by many of what historically has been happening on the face of the earth for centuries.

The book of Revelation was written around the close of the first century of the Christian era. The Horsemen rode together. What is the meaning of this for us today? It is hoped this book will provide some answers.

Attempts have been made by researchers to classify famine according to who is affected and where the affected population is located. For instance, *general famine* affects all classes or groups within the country or region of food shortage, although often not all the groups of people suffer to the same degree. Whereas, *regional famine* is concentrated in only part of a country, but all groups within the region of shortage are usually affected.

Class famine, on the other hand, describes a condition in which certain population groups suffer the greatest hardship in a country short of food, regardless of the geographic concentration of the famine. While the causes of famine are numerous, they are usually divided into natural and human categories and they may affect different groups of people within a country or region.

Natural or Physical Causes

Natural or physical causes of famine destroy crops and food supplies largely through drought, heavy rain and flooding, of unseasonably cold weather, typhoons, vermin depradations, plant disease and insect infestations.

Drought is the most easily understood natural cause and the prime contributor to famine in arid and semiarid regions. But drought may occur outside the region affected. Sometimes drought in the headwaters of a major river used for irrigation can cause famine in an irrigated region downstream. History records the earliest famines as dating back to the 4th millennium B.C. and occurring in ancient Egypt and the Middle East. Egypt was also afflicted with locust plagues.

Such early famines have been called physical famines because of the natural environment's general hostility to intensive sedentary agriculture.

History shows that ancient China and India felt the disastrous results of drought because of their primitve agriculture and inadequate means of transportation—a combination that still brings famine problems to many places in the world.

Actually, since 1700 Asia has been the principal, but not the only, famine region of the world. Overpopulation is a word you hear used frequently when famine is discussed. Too many people; too many babies being born. (There are reasons for the babies. I discuss this in another chapter.)

Overpopulation, however, has not been nor is it the sole contributor to famine. While overpopulation poses a real risk, actually there is sufficient food in the world today. It is one of the myths surrounding famine's causes. Population experts have long predicted an increased pressure of population unchecked that might be expected to breed increased famines worldwide. Such chilling glimpses into the future do bring prognostications of things to come that should make us more sensitive to the world's hunger problem. In 1977 the United Nations estimated that 460 million people were going to bed hungry every night. In 1989 that figure stood at 1 billion. And, at best, these are only guesstimates.

When famine occurs in these densely populated drought- and flood-prone areas, agricultural production is already at or barely above the subsistence level. India and China are notable examples where overpopulation famine has occured. Recorded famine in India dates to the 14th century and continues in the 20th.

India, whose rivers play a crucial role in maintaining its agricultural lands, is heavily dependent upon rainfall. Even the emperors were unable to provide the barest necessities for their households in the great Indian famines.

There was no rainfall at all during the terrible years of 1660 and 1661 on the Indian subcontinent.

There was a famine in Deccan, India (1702-04) that was reportedly responsible for the deaths of about 2 million persons. In contrast, jumping far beyond that, the 1965 drought-caused famine recorded in Bihar saw thousands dying, not millions, because of the tremendous success of relief operations.

More than 10 million people, a third of the total population of Bengal, are said to have perished during the famine of 1769-70. It was said of this famine that the air was "so infected by the noxious effluvia of dead bodies" and rent by cries of the dying that few dared venture on the streets.

More than 5 million persons died between 1876 and 1878 in Bombay, Madras and Mysore, despite frantic but pitifully inadequate attempts to prevent it. In more recent years, another Bengal famine (1943) is reported to have taken the lives of 1.5 million people. Ten famines are reported as occurring in India between 1860 and 1900 with an estimated 15 million deaths.

A look at Appendix B in this book will provide a relatively complete rundown of the major historical famines from c.3500 B.C. through 1983 A.D.

In 1876-79, an estimated 9 million to 13 million persons died during a famine that swept over northern China. "The people's faces are black with hunger; they are dying by thousands upon thousands," reported a Western traveler. "Women and girls and boys are openly offered for sale to any chance wayfarer. . .A respectable married woman could be easily bought for six dollars, and a little girl for two. . .Parents have been known to kill their children sooner than witness their prolonged sufferings, killing themselves afterwards."

Famine continued to plague China into the 20th century with more than 3 million persons starving to death in 1928-29. A study at Nanking University revealed that from 108 B.C. to A.D. 1911 there were 1,828 famines in China, or nearly one somewhere every year. The 1958 to 1961 famine in China, the largest in history is said to have cost the lives of from 16 to 30 million people.

Human Causes

Human causes for famine are primarily political and cultural in nature. Unlike most natural causes, they are within the bounds of human control. This, of course, is where man's inhumanity to man enters the picture.

Famines were common in medieval Europe. At one time,

peasant farmers living in isolated and self-sufficing communities formed the majority of the population, so that a crop failure in one locality meant famine even if harvests not too far away were normal.

Records are not always accurate, of course, so there is some variance as you research for historical information and statistics. One report says 450 recorded famines occured in Europe from the year 1000 to 1855 and were largely confined to small local regions such as Wales, Lorraine and Alsace; another study says 600 famines were recorded from 6 A.D. to 1855.

These were major famines, dirths caused by long cold winters, which hindered planting, or by dry or cold summers, which prevented growth, and by floods, locusts and war. The latter indicates once again the human cause for suffering .

The severe and prolonged food shortages of Roman times have been characterized as transportation famines. Rome was, at times, unable to transport food to regions of shortage; but often she was unwilling. Grain equaled wealth for the emperors. To hoard grain while regions of the empire suffered was a common practice. The Roman famine of 436 B.C. is well documented. Thousands of persons committed suicide by throwing themselves into the Tiber River to escape the pain of starvation.

The development of large urban populations in Greece and Rome increased the difficulties of securing sufficient food in years of bad harvests.

Egypt, which depends on the Nile River and its fertile delta for its agriculture, suffered many similar severe episodes. Possibly none was worse than the great famine of A.D. 42 during which a great part of its population was wiped out.

In 1889, when the British made war in the Sudan, a plague of locusts swarmed over the fields beside the Nile. They carpeted roads and farms a foot deep, stripping the grain bare. Many of the starving Egyptians turned to cannibalism. Others perished in the streets or on the banks of the Nile. It was reported that the waters were black with bodies.

Cultural Food Shortages

European famines have been characterized as cultural food shortages. Natural causes played a role in famines of the Middle Ages, but it was the feudal social system, cultural practices, and overpopulation that extended food shortages into malnutrition, widespread disease and famine.

A report from the year 1123 states that the English "let lifeless bodies lie unburied in cities, villages and crossroads." Despair and the stench of death were everywhere.

Actually, during the Middle Ages, the British Isles were afflicted by at least 95 famines, and France suffered the effects of 75 or more. In 1235 some 20,000 London residents died from famine, and many resorted to eating tree bark for survival—a not uncommon practice in many places even today. When the edible leaves of trees have been stripped and eaten, and there is nothing else, this is what happens.

Italy has known famine. In the Italy of A.D. 450 starving parents ate their children. During an Irish famine in A.D. 963, desperate parents went as far as trading their children for food.

Russia was scourged by major famines eleven times between 1845 and 1922. Drought was seen as the culprit causing crop failures, but the steadily increasing population and progressively smaller farms contributed. The peasant population has always suffered even in normal times from lack of food because of the primitive agricultural methods, and as a result in 1890 the death rate was higher by 30 percent in rural districts than for Russia as a whole.

When adequate reserves cannot be maintained, even a partial crop failure is a major disaster and precipitates famine conditions regardless of the region or locale.

The 1921-22 famine in the Soviet Union was blamed, among other things, on an international blockade against the country.

The potato fungus blight of Ireland (1846-51) resulted in the deaths of 2 to 3 million either from starvation or the pestilence that followed it. The famine was intensified by the miserable poverty of the people who were dependent on potatoes for sustenance. This was the most disastrous famine in western Europe in the 19th century. It resulted in the massive emigration to the United States of an estimated million and a half within a decade.

Speaking of America and the New World on this continent, one known instance of famine occurred about 1051 whereby the Toltecs were forced to migrate from a stricken region in what is now Central Mexico.

Scholars generally agree that the more diverse New World food sources and, in the case of the Incas, an extensive food storage system which they had, mitigated the effects of famine.

New World populations, it is felt, were less sedentary than Old World peoples, and migration for them was not as forbidding. The Toltecs and the Indians of Mesa Verde (now in Colorado, U.S.) apparently did this with success.

The American story of the infamous Donner exploration party is one of the more tragic stories of the settling of the West. The Donner Pass is a 7,088 foot mountain pass cutting through the Sierra Nevadas in eastern California through which a party of 82 settlers from Illinois and adjoining states, led by George and Jacob Donner, became snowbound. Only 47 survived. They built crude shelters of logs, rocks and hides, and ate twigs, mice, their animals, their shoes, and finally their own dead. It is a sad blot on American history that we do not like to dwell on, but it happened because people were faced with starvation.

Warfare: The Most Human Cause of Famine

But, once again, let me emphasize that my research shows that warfare has been the most common human cause of famine. And this is what is of such concern to me.

Not only are crops and food supplies destroyed, seized, transported out of a country, or kept, confiscated by ruthless rebels and fighting insurgents depriving the people of access to even minimum bare necessities for survival, but warfare also disrupts the distribution of food through the use of siege and blockade tactics. War is merciless.

History has remarkably recorded man's inhumanity to man through using food and starvation in scorched-earth policies.

The famines that plagued eastern Europe between 1500 and 1700 were political. The political aspirations of eastern European countries interfered in and often controlled the production and distribution of basic foodstuffs. In addition to warfare, natural causes continued to play a part in famine during this period.

Famines in Hungary in 1505 and 1586 drove some parents to eat their children. And Russia was not spared from the effects of famine during this period. In 1600 some half-million people died of starvation in Russia.

Deliberate destruction of crops and food supplies was a common tactic of war in the 19th century, employed by both attacking and defending armies. For instance, the scorched-earth policy adopted by the Russians in 1812 not only deprived Napolean's armies of needed food, but did the same to the Russian people.

But nothing approaches for sheer savagery the infamous policies of the German Third Reich between 1933 and 1945. A closer look at this and other such atrocities in our generation is examined in the next chapter.

What we must not forget is that behind all these grim statistics, stories and definitions have been and are ordinary people—men, women, young people, children and infants —caught in the vicious circumstances of persistent hunger.

4 War and Hunger: A Harrowing Catalogue of Human Misery

Throughout history hunger has known no law.

Wholesale human extermination. That's what happens in war when hunger is used as the weapon. War is both a cause of famine and a means employed to overcome it. Throughout history hunger has known no law.

I find it awesome to consider that the number of people starving today, at this very moment, is greater than the total population of the earth at the time of the American Revolution. I repeat, to me that's awesome.

A century ago a famine in the Sudan, clearly caused by government and warring rebels, would have received very little new's coverage worldwide. Today, however, television drops the news starkly visible, right into millions of living rooms. Rapid progress in media communications has heightened awareness throughout the world of the problems and the suffering of humans in faroff places. A social consciousness now exists that did not exist to quite the extent it does today.

Whether it's via the print media, or telephone/telex/ satellite systems, together with the use of computerized data, that brings us the news, no longer can the world plead ignorance. Distance, national boundaries, ethnic consideration. . .they are no longer hindering factors in the face of the stark reality of the horrors of world hunger, whatever the cause, whether it be a Hurricane Gilbert slamming into the island of Jamaica, floodwaters devastating Bangladesh, an earthquake in Afghanistan, or the "silent war" of Southern Sudan.

"The Silent Wars"

Call it by whatever name you wish, but the planned starvation of whole populations is one of the cruelest schemes ever devised by godless men.

Some of us lived through World War II. We can recall the news reports as they filtered through. But at the conclusion of the war, when the atrocities of the German Third Reich were revealed in all their unimaginable, unthinkable horror, the conscience of millions was deeply stirred. *How could this have happened in a world supposedly civilized?*

Recently a memorandum relating to planned starvation came to my attention. It was a secret memo dated May 1, 1941, seven weeks before the German invasion of the U.S.S.R., which stated: "There is no doubt that as a result, many millions of persons will be starved to death, if we take out of the country the things necessary for us." [1]

The Nazi governor of the Warsaw district in Poland is quoted as having said in 1941, upon the sealing of the nine square miles of that city that were to house half a million Jews: "Jews will disappear because of hunger and need, and nothing will remain of the Jewish question but a cemetery." [2] And it was almost true—only a few hundred survived after a month of fighting prior to the ghetto's total liquidation, on May 16, 1943.

It is impossible to give an account of all the crimes committed by the Nazis in occupied Poland. Mass uprooting of population, bombing of objects of art, sending people to labor camps, biological extermination of nations, political, religious and racial persecution, mass arrests, torturing of prisoners, mass executions—these were only some among a whole series of their crimes.

The reign of terror in Poland resulted in the deaths of 6 million Polish citizens. It was met with valiant resistance on the part of resistance movement organizations.

Concentration Camps

The Nazis built a network of concentration camps, the number of which, together with sub-camps established chiefly in the vicinity of munition plants, amounted to over one thousand in 1944. The biggest among them was the concentration camp Auschwitz-Birkenau.

Besides concentration camps, extermination camps were established at Treblinka, Belzec, Chelmno, Sobibor. According to statistics, compiled after the war, about 10 million people perished in all Nazi camps.[3]

I visited Auschwitz in Poland. As we entered the former concentration camp, deserted watch towers no longer displayed machine guns, the shouts of the guards were not heard, nor did I hear the trampling of sentries' boots at the times of the changing of the guard. Thousands of emaciated prisoners, clad in striped prison clothes, no longer haunted the world's greatest battlefield—for such Auschwitz certainly had been considering that all told it is believed 4 million persons from all the countries under Nazi occupation perished there.[4]

Among those who perished in these camps were priests and members of various religious denominations, men and women belonging to various social strata and professions. Healthy or sick, young or old, they shared the same fate in the extermination factories in the big gas chambers and crematories built just for this purpose. We saw those ovens. Our guide was a man whose father and brother were executed there. As we saw these ovens where humans were burned, the gas chambers were innumerable, and I knew we were seeing the ravages of hate and demon power.

As for food, the daily rations included only the following: Breakfast—½ litre of black coffee or tea with 5 grammes of sugar at the very most; Noon—soup consisting of potatoes, turnips or cabbage with a minimum content of meat or fat, it was dished out at noon and most often had to be eaten cold at night. All sorts of waste material would be found in the soup, e.g., buttons, pieces of paper. Supper consisted of ½ litre of coffee or "herbs," one piece of bread, sausage or margarine (these items varied from day to day). Sometimes on Fridays a prisoner would receive 5-6 middle-sized boiled potatoes. The constantly increasing calorie deficiency led to starvation sickness. After the initial fat reserves stored in the body had been used up, death became inevitable.[5]

The prisoners in this state of protracted starvation were called "moslems" in the jargon of the camp. Their bones were barely covered with skin, their eyes glazed and vacant. In advanced stages of starvation they moved slowly because they lacked the strength to carry the weight of their body frame. Apathy and somnolence were the characteristic symptoms of starvation. Complete physical decline went together with mental exhaustion, typified by extreme indifference to, and lack of interest in their surroundings. These prisoners found it impossible to concentrate their thoughts, their memory failed them to such an extent that they were unable to even remember their names.[6]

And you have to remember that they were required to do incredibly hard physical labor in all kinds of weather for which they were not clothed properly. Besides that, they were beaten and suffered inhumane torture, their living quarters were indescribably filthy, damp and cold in the winter, or hot in the summer. Most of the time they slept on rotting and stinking straw on the floor. If they did have sleeping berths, an average of eight people used one berth for "sleeping." One prisoner described it like this: "The stink, thirst and hunger made sleep impossible."

As to sanitary conditions, they were practically non-existant. The "hospitals" were overcrowded, there was insufficient equipment and a lack of drugs, so that the hospital actually became "an anteroom to the crematorium." In addition, SS doctors conducted illegal experiments upon prisoners with the view of learning surgery by using living bodies.

The process of extermination, together with other aspects of life in a concentration camp, were top secret, but one member of a special squad managed to make notes of several tragic events. He hid them in a glass jar and then buried them underground. Among them mention is made of the killing of children:

> The children were so pretty, so well-made that it was striking, when compared with the rags they were covered with. It happened in the second half of October 1944. The children had noticed the smoke from the chimney and realized they were being led to their death. They began running hither and thither in the yard, in a dead fright, clutching their heads in despair.

As I left that horrible place, I couldn't help thinking to myself that those millions of innocent people, including children, had no way to exit other than through the crematorium chimney. And I have gone to the trouble of telling you all this to make you aware of the terrible things that have gone on in this world and are, in fact, going on in many places on this globe. Not mass exterminations by gassing and crematoriums anymore, but nutritional discrimination, and death by hunger and its awful results. Food deprivation the weapon. The adversary is on the prowl.

Nutritional Discrimination

Deliberately, with planned precision, in cold blood, these less than human men of war and greed, exterminated tens of millions by campaigns of starvation. In truth, nutritional discrimination became the handmaiden of racial discrimination as Slavic and Jewish humans perished in the process.

Who can forget that great Dutch lady, Corrie Ten Boom, who emerged from the horrors of Ravensbruck Concentration Camp following the war, to become, in her words, "A tramp for the Lord," as she crisscrossed the globe telling of what happened to prisoners of war like herself. She was a survivor, but tens of thousands of her countrymen, including her own sister, never made it—victims of enforced labor, starvation and the effects of malnutrition.

The loss of life in the U.S.S.R. (1932-34; and the siege of Leningrad between November 1941 and April 1942), Greece (1941-43) and Poland (1941-42) due to causes aggravated by hunger and malnutrition, and increased mortality and reduced births, runs into the multimillions.

War and civil disorder in this century have caused famine in the Congo (1960-61), Biafra (1967-68), Kampuchea (1975-79), Ethiopia (1984). Ethiopia suffered greatly in 1973 also because of a severe drought that caused an estimated loss of life of 100,000 people. Emperor Haile Selassie did not want to spoil tourist trade and so he would not allow the famine to be publicized, thus cutting off foreign aid.

Much of the loss of life that results is directly traceable to epidemics and kwashiorkor which is a form of malnutrition in children and infants caused by a diet that may contain carbohydrates but lacks protein. This is very common in countries such as the Congo and Biafra (Nigeria).

The Invisible Killer

History records how the pressure of population on food supplies causes more powerful groups to raid or seize the fertile valleys and plains from better-fed neighbors. Through the centuries many different peoples raided the fertile valleys of the Euphrates, the Nile, the Danube, the Rhine, the Volga, the Indus, the Ganges, and the Yangtze. Scottish Highlanders raided the Lowlands to the south; and even the Pilgrims in America, driven by hunger, raided the food supplies of the Indians. Sometimes these raiders were small groups, sometimes they were armies of millions. Oftentimes it was and is accompanied by the forced movements of people, we call them "refugees," displaced persons uprooted from their land, their homes, their countries, forced to flee for their lives. But the word *refugee* itself is synonymous with hunger.

But regardless how many or how few, the end result was and is suffering and great loss of life. Hunger, the invisible killer, accomplishing its deadly work again.

Victimized people are all too easily decimated by hunger and exhaustion.

---

1. Nuremberg Trials, Nazi Conspiracy and Aggression, Memorandum of Meeting V, p. 378 (N.D. 2718-PS), quoted in W.L. Shirer, *The Rise and Fall of the Third Reich* (New York: Simon & Schuster, 1960), p. 833.

2. J. Apenszlak, ed., *The Black Book of Polish Jewry* (New York: American Federation for Polish Jews in Cooperation with Association of Jewish Refugees and Immigrants from Poland, 1943), p. 22.

3. Kazimerz Smolen, *Auschwitz 1940-1945 Guidebook Through the Museum* (Krajowa Agencja Wydawnicza, 1981), pp. 17-19.

4. The number was arrived at as the result of computations made after surveying the terrain, the installations of destruction and the documents of the Auschwitz camp; it is also based upon the evidence of surviving prisoners and upon the opinion of experts. Three international organizations investigated the Auschwitz camp situation and all reported the same thing, that "no less than 4 million people perished in Auschwitz." Those organizations were: The Soviet State Extraordinary Commission for the Investigation of Nazi Crimes, The Supreme National Tribunal in Poland, and The International Military Tribunal in Nuremberg.

5. Ibid., pp 58-59.

6. Ibid., p. 59.

5 Driven People: Earth's Hungry Wanderers

Refugee: *A displaced person who is the victim of social unrest, intolerance, natural disasters, or war.*

Jesus was a refugee before the age of two.

Have you ever stopped to think about that? It was an angel of the Lord who appeared to Joseph in a dream telling him to get up and to flee with Mary and Jesus to Egypt. "Remain there till I tell you [otherwise]; for Herod intends to search for the Child in order to destroy Him" (Matthew 2:13 AMP).

Now it's true that they didn't flee because they were hungry, but they quite literally became displaced persons. In this instance they were told explicitly to go to Egypt.

The Old Testament accounts of Abraham moving from Ur, and then later of Jacob and his sons settling in Egypt to escape the famine in Canaan, show people on the move though for different reasons. It isn't always wanderlust that compels people to roam the world, often it has to do with a search for food. Of course the dramatic story of Jacob, Joseph and the brothers hinges on hunger—when famine struck not only Egypt where Joseph was prime minster, but all surrounding countries as well. "When the famine was over all the land, Joseph opened all the storehouses, and sold to the Egyptians; for the famine grew extremely distressing in the land of Egypt. And all countries came to Egypt to Joseph to buy grain, because the famine was severe over all [the known] earth" (Genesis 41:56-57).

No One Chooses to be a Refugee

Dispossession—becoming hungry travelers—causes emotional suffering as well as physical. Imagine leaving behind your livelihood. Many, for instance, who became expellees in Europe during the Second World War, left behind farms that had been fruitfully cultivated for countless generations. Barracks, requisitioned schools, and warehouses were jampacked with men and women dragooned into forced labor in ammunition factories and farms.

In the aftermath of the Second World War, an estimated forty million refugees were in the world with the most massive presence being on the European continent. The weakest among the expelled people clung precariously on the edges of life, but in the end many perished. The chronicles of death coming out of war-torn Europe, in particular at the hands of the Nazis, were tales of horror and sadness. This is a sorry episode in modern world history.

The fate of the uprooted never makes for pleasant reading.

Refugee camps provide only a minimum of that which is needed for survival. Usually the water supply is scant in addition to the food rations, and always there is the problem of inadequate sanitary facilities. Life is grim. No one chooses to be a refugee. Hunger, for most, is acute.

Whether they are displaced persons from Europe, South Vietnam, Korea, Cambodia, Tibet, Palestine, or Africa, their lives are empty, made so by grinding poverty, pervading hunger, soul-killing boredom, and shameful dependency. They are people who have no place to call home and no hope.

Some of us have a hard time trying to sort all this out. To bring it closer to home, try to imagine the combined populations of many states in America being uprooted and people having to scramble over state boundaries with nothing but the clothes on their backs and perhaps a cooking pot or a few other meager, hastily gathered belongings. Then think about what this would do to the the adjoining states where they try to settle. Mass migrations pose enormous problems not only to those migrating, but to the countries into which they flee.

For instance, when ten million unwanted and burdensome Bengali refugees staggered into India in almost one wave, what was India to do? Her eastern states of West Bengal, Bihar and Meghalaya were already overcrowded. She was already faced with chronic food shortages for her own people, now what was Mother India to do with these uninvited waifs of a civil war? The result was, as history records, that India had to attack the Pakistani army in Bangladesh so that the territory could open up and reverse the tide of refugees. All sorts of consequences are the result of dispersion in a shoulder-to-shoulder world.

The Man-made Disaster of the Refugee

Nothing strikes me as being so heartbreaking as the uprooting of peoples, whole villages, entire large areas, forced to leave behind their possessions, and to set out on foot for where? Wandering nomads becoming, as it were, a nation of the nationless. Oh, the injustice of it all! Refugees, the uprooting of people as a causative factor of hunger. For it is so true, refugees cannot produce food.

Refugees only bring themselves and increased need to areas where food and water are already in short supply. They stagger out of the bush, wearing scraps of bark or sacking or nothing at all, arriving at overcrowded refugee camps. They tell of mass executions, razing of whole villages, forced labor, systematic rape and beatings, and starvation.

The Arithmetic of Refugees and Hunger

Figures vary, the arithmetic of the refugee problem is not easily figured. Refugees, distributed over a vast area of the earth's surface, are part of the world's greatest problem as we approach the twenty-first century. Victimized by war, social unrest or political decisions, they vote for life with the only ballot left to them—their feet.

I wonder, does anyone still remember the anger and confusion that raged through one of the largest refugee camps in the world, Hong Kong, as the mainland Chinese ran from Communism? They lived in unbelievable conditions.

Our family lived in Hong Kong when more refugees were shot than survived.

Today Hong Kong is a thriving metropolis. But who remembers that it was the incredibly industrious Chinese who made this rocky colony into a beehive of production for the world at large?

Escape by Sea: Escape by Air

Americans felt the challenge of the refugee in April 1975 when a new generation of refugees was born in Vietnam with the fall of Saigon. Thousands of Vietnamese were helicoptered out of Saigon while thousands took to the sea from Vietnam's long coastline.

This 1975 exodus led to the open sea. How treacherous! How sad! Escapees were saved by ships of many flags and airlifted to the U.S. There was a brief period when 140,000 Vietnamese were housed in Army forts throughout the U.S. One researcher tells of talking with some of the Vietnamese awaiting resettlement in Pennsylvania. For many, it was the second experience of uprooting within two decades. But through a computer terminal operating at Fort Indiantown Gap, Pennsylvania, relatives all over the United States were being reunited. It was the first instance when computer technology was utilized to bring together families whom the application of war technology had scattered.[1]

America: The Country of First Asylum for a New Surge of Refugees

The United States became the country of first asylum for three hundred thousand uprooted people from the area known as Indo-China.

But we also became the refuge for Cubans and Haitians who arrived in Florida in flotillas of every type of craft from tiny fishing boats to small yachts. The Cuban influx made front page headlines, and the problems of the refugee made the evening news. We learned once again the difficulties of assimilating the uprooted who arrived with nothing but their needs and their expectations.

In this country, when emergency situations arise of this magnitude, the government is quick to declare an area a "disaster area," thus making it eligible for federal funds. Florida came under that designation when it found itself the haven port for these refugees.

The Ongoing Problems of the "Boat People"

Fleeing refugees from Vietnam came to be known as the "boat people." But as the mounting tide of these people came to receiving areas such as Singapore and Malaysia, these poorer countries found they simply could not supply the encampments of refugees that were growing on their shorelines. Horror stories of cases of boatloads of famished people being towed out to sea abound. Many of these rickety, old boats fell apart under the strain of their overload and the people drowned at sea.

Hong Kong was forced to reopen its "DP Camps" (Displaced Persons Camps) for close to seventy thousand refugees from Vietnam.

International pipelines which had saved many thousands of earlier refugees, now had to be reopened.

Thailand also became a country of first asylum for many Vietnamese refugees fleeing from a new regime, but also for Kampucheans (formerly Cambodians) fleeing from a "murderous Utopia." The atrocities that happened with the "liberation" of Phnom Penh are now legendary, imposed by a few Marxist ideologues bent on forcibly overthrowing all existing social conditions. Banks were shut down, currency outlawed, schools closed, hospitals emptied of patients who were deposited on roads leading to the countryside. Not only did thousands die on the roadsides, but a systematic liquidation of "class enemies" was carried out. Before it was all over, an estimated two to three million Kampucheans were dead. It was likened to the mass death of the Jews in Europe's holocaust.

Added to the senseless killings and sufferings imposed on the innocent, were the effects of the monsoon rains that came. Along with that came sickness and hunger. Relief and international rescue efforts helped greatly in offsetting the suffering and loss of life. But Thailand became a country overrun with refugees living in hastily constructed shelters of corrugated iron, thatch, plastic, tarpaulins—anything that could be found. The most helpless of these refugees, as in any refugee camps, were the unaccompanied children, most of whom had lost their parents during the escape, first by land and then by sea.

The UN and voluntary relief agencies had the monstrous task of channeling food and supplies to these desperately needy people, and then helping them to find places to resettle. They dispersed to the United States, France, Canada and Australia, in that order, with the remainder finding places in thirty other countries. But before that happened, bizarre lifesaving operations were conducted month after month in what had become a "no-man's land" where continuing chaos occurred. But the flexibility of voluntary agencies and religious groups was shown time after time in meeting these needs.

A Continuing Refugee Presence

Africa has had to adapt to a continuing refugee presence in many of her countries. From Angola to Mozambique, from the Sudan or Nigeria, Zimbabwe, Malawi, Guinea, Zaire, Uganda, Chad or South Africa, the situation is always grave and explosive with violent overturnings of regimes and great civil strife. And always there is a shortage of water and food.

Somalia, for instance, presented to the world a face of agony more intense than anything in recent African history (except perhaps for the emaciated civilians of Biafra, so many of whom perished during the 1960s). Somalia is considered one of the world's least developed nations and one of the half dozen poorest countries on the earth in terms of per capita income. Yet in the arithmetic of poverty, hunger and suffering, the total of refugees in makeshift camps in the country reached one million. And these "camps" were nothing more than flimsy brush huts thatched with grass. Sixty percent were children, 30 percent were women, and only 10 percent were males (many of them aged), yet they set to work and dug wells and did what had to be done to try and survive.

Again, it was voluntary and Christian relief agencies who came to the rescue. It was the compassion of the citizenry of the world who made such rescue efforts possible. The question always persists, however, where will these refugees go to find livelihood? What will they do? The persistence of hunger as a reality and of long duration must be recognized by those of us in places throughout the world where we have it within our power to help alleviate suffering.[2]

I read the statistics coming out of the southern Sudan, for instance, where I learn that 6 million civilians are being used as pawns. Six million human beings in one part of the world alone! During five years of war, a third of southern Sudan's civilian population was put to flight in northern Sudan and neighboring Ethiopia. But what of the remaining 4 million suffering people? They are either holed up with the army in major southern cities and towns, or they roam the countryside, trying to avoid looting and attacks by rebels.

Think about it. How would you like it if suddenly you realized if you didn't grab what you could carry, and didn't gather your loved ones around you hurriedly explaining the need to run for your lives, that unless you did, you might be tortured to death, forced to join enemy forces, your women and little girls taken as slaves? What would that do to you?

Or how would you feel, as the male head of your household, if your wife, sisters, and little girls were raped before your eyes? Then, at gun or spear point, you had to leave them behind as your captors marched you off with them and you knew you would be forced to fight and kill your fellow countrymen?

As you stagger along, with one last backward glance at your loved ones and your village, you carry with you the memory of the older villagers, perhaps even your parents, being killed, the village burning, your womenfolk kidnapped, crying out for mercy, knowing they will be forced into a life of servitude. Everything has been plundered. No food has been left for them. How will they survive? What will they do? Where will they go?

This is an all-too-common scene with some variations. It's been going on for years in various places throughout the world. The survivors become people without a homeland, victims who have had no control over their destiny. Casualties of man's inhumanity to man.

We have met these people. We have been with them in their displaced condition in refugee camps. We have seen the looks on their faces, the rags on their bodies, the meager possessions in their huts and tents. I have yet to hear one of them complain.

We have also talked with them in the hospitals and in a Nicaraguan resistance recovery center. We saw young boys and men who had been wounded in the battles between the Contras and the Sandinistas who were recovering. Some of these boys were as young as twelve years old, but they were preparing to go back and fight for freedom from the Sandinistas' oppression. I marveled at their courage.

The stories we heard at this recovery center were heartbreaking. They were all-too-typical accounts, I knew, of what happens when people lose everything they have, including loved ones, and have to flee for their lives. These wounded escapees from the terror in their homeland of Nicaragua had battled to survive in the depths of the jungle as they made their way to Costa Rica for hospitalization. Many never made it. Those who did subsisted on roots, berries, leaves and grubs. In a time of famine hungry people will eat anything, even the earth itself, which contains some nutrients from which a starving person, in his desperation, can draw a limited amount of nourishment. One thing humans cannot live on is grass, our digestive apparatus will not permit us to draw sustenance from cellulos as cattle, sheep, goats, deer and some other animals can do. But these refugees come straggling into the already over-crowded refugee camps, walking skeletons.

We talked to one young man who showed us where a bullet entered through his nose, took a curve and went down into his lung. He knew that it had destroyed something in-side and he immediately began to pray. As he prayed, he began to vomit, and vomited up the bullet. But one lung was destroyed and had to be removed. He showed us where the surgeon had to make an incision from his back and side around to the front and stomach. But he was making a recovery at the recovery center.

A young boy, twelve years old, told us he had gone to war alongside his father. He saw his father tortured and killed by the Sandinistas, and he was wounded, but he escaped during the same battle. Amazingly, he survived the trek to the recovery center. He told me he knew God had a purpose for his life in sparing him.

A fine-looking nineteen-year-old with an amputated leg told me he wanted to go back, but knew he couldn't. I saw many like him with missing limbs, men without eyes, men who have been shot in various parts of the body. Most of these men were assisted to a truck and taken to a hospital in Costa Rica. But they had to leave their families behind. They don't know if their loved ones are dead or alive.

All these men had the same message: Ask the people

to pray for their families, their friends and their country.

Freedom is dear to these people; they don't take it for granted. They have suffered terribly.

An Unwinnable War

One of our American pastor-directors, Tennyson Fitch from Indiana, talked to the mayor of a community near the Nicaraguan border whose pastor-father had been assassinated by the communists in 1983 because he was preaching the Gospel. He expressed deep gratitude for the food we brought. "They come across the border," he explained, "fleeing for their lives, without money, they have no contact with their families, and if it wasn't for God's people reaching out with a helping hand, they would be utterly lost and without hope in the world."

I find myself asking this question over and over again: How would you like it, Lester, if you were faced with the option of being imprisoned or killed if you would not accept the Communism ideology? Your only option would be to fall in line with what your captors demanded, or to try to escape.

Repression, hunger and suffering are the daily lot of these people. We were able to assure these victims of such injustice that they were not forgotten people.

Waves of Desperate People

Whether it's southern Sudan and Ethiopia, or the Mozambican refugees fleeing the cruelty of war, crowding into the tiny country of Malawi, hundreds of thousands stumble across the borders into neighboring countries, waves of desperate people.

Relief organizations and the governments of countries taking in these pathetic people, struggle to provide food and services for the refugees. But at the same time they are trying to ease acute food shortages, they are often fighting insect infestations and pockets of drought in their own countries.

And always there is disease. Sickness and disease. Their bodies are covered with sores. Malnutrition always exacerbates the effects of undernourishment, especially in young children. Diarrhea and dysentry, edema, worms, cholera, severe coughing, pnuemonia, bronchitis, measles outbreaks. . . There are no rest rooms in most refugee camps. People have been stripped of all dignity. The health hazard that is created is unbelievable. The people often are unable to control their bodily functions. Everyone is barefoot. Can you begin to imagine what it is like, walking in human excrement, the stench overwhelming?

And where do these humans sleep? Such camps seldom have enough tents. Often there are no blankets.

The weather? Wind. Extremes of cold and/or hot. Dust. Parched ground.

Such is the life of the refugee.

Africa's Worst Refugee Crisis

War, hunger, poverty, disease. Their property looted, destroyed, plundered. Soap? What is that? Food? Clothing? Some of these victims had known creature comforts, but now they have nothing. Along with others they find themselves a part of incredible human congestion on land already crowded. The refugees know they are severely stretching health, water and other services in countries that are already stretched, and where child mortality and malnutrition are among the highest in the world. But what are they to do? All around them they see severe land degradation and deforestation as trees have been cut down for fuel, building materials, and to eat (bark and leaves).

One newspaper release said more than 220,000 Mozambicans had settled in the southern tip of Malawi, which has the largest concentration of refugees in Africa, and they outnumbered the local population by at least 30,000. And still they were pouring in, naked and weak from such ailments as malaria, bilharzia, diarrhea, severe malnutrition and leprosy. This same release told of a farmer who arrived at a refugee reception center wearing a dirty grain sack as clothing. He had walked for three days with his seven-year-old daughter to reach even this patch of sandy ground. His farm had been plundered and in making their getaway, he and his wife ran in different directions. His wife had three of the children, he ran with one. Would they ever see each other again?

U.S. News & World Report (May 2, 1988) spoke of "The killing fields of Mozambique," and the "rebels without a cause serving South Africa by wreaking havoc." Some have said these rebels may be today's most brutal rebel army.

But the stories are the same, wherever they come from. A State Department researcher who collected refugee testimonies by visiting 25 camps in Mozambique and four neighboring countries, pointed to a pattern of atrocities more vicious and more mindless than anything the world has seen since Cambodia's Khmer Rogue.

The refugee accounts include killings by shooting

bayoneting, axing, burning alive, smothering, forced starvation and drowning.

Typical of the effects of displacement and fleeing for one's life is the story I heard of a Mali herdsman who lost his cattle to drought and then led his family on a grueling 200-mile trek to the nearest refugee camp. When they finally staggered into the camp, they found that emergency rations had been largely exhausted by crowds of refugees already there. A relief worker managed to supply them with four minimal, children's portions of gruel. But there were five children in the family.

"My wife and I will go without," the man said impassively. Then his voice broke. "But how can I decide which of my five children shall starve?"

In the final analysis, the worldwide refugee tragedy comes down to the question this father asked. Who shall starve? Who is to survive?

---

1. William Byron, *The Causes of World Hunger* (Ramsey, N.J.: The Paulist Press, 1982), the chapter entitled "Refugees: The Uprooting of Peoples as a Cause of Hunger" by Eileen Egan.

2. Much of the information in this chapter was gleaned from the previously mentioned book.

6 A Dark Hole of Death for Babies and Children

Do you hear the children weeping, O my brothers. . .
the young, young children? O my brothers.
They are weeping bitterly!
They are weeping in the playtime of the others.[1]

On the average, 24 people die of hunger every minute, and 18 of them are children. The yearly estimated global number of children who die of hunger is 15 million. But remember, these are only estimates. I am convinced the number must be much higher.

They aren't just statistics. They are babies and children. Real life little people. Yet, somehow, tragically the way they are referred to in some literature you almost get the impression that they are being used as pawns. We see them marketed in almost a casual way through the pathetic pictures of Third World country children with their matchstick legs, distended stomachs, and soulful eyes.

These tiny victims of hunger and malnutrition's related diseases are not just pictures used in attractive brochures designed to tug at your heartstrings. They are so very real and even though we, and others, use these photos, I am convinced for the most part it is not done in a casual, indifferent way. This is what we have seen. This is what our cameras have recorded. There is no pretty way to portray the face of suffering caused by hunger.

One of the best indicators of hunger is considered the infant mortality rate (IMR), which tells how many children per thousand die before their first birthday. Again, statistics vary, but statistics released by the World Bank in 1984 show that about 125 million children are born each year, of these some 18 million (14.5 percent) will not see their fifth birthday. And of those who die, 97 percent were born in Third World countries.

Women and children, especially female children, are always the first casualties of hunger. Although globally speaking more boys than girls die during their first year of life, in many Third World societies, more baby girls die than boys since boys are given more food than their sisters especially when there's not enough to go around to begin with.

Women are considered biologically to be tougher than men. The explanation is set forth that nature wants to safeguard the uterus for future generations. But social structures in the Third World put to an end any advantage conferred on women. The reason for this is obvious if you know anything about the culture in these Third World countries. Women do most of the hard work. We saw this when we distributed heavy sacks of maize meal in Zimbabwe at a place called Binga. It was the women and girls who took these heavy bags, hoisted them to their heads and walked off smiling and very grateful. Women in these countries work at least two-thirds of all the hours, but they get only one-tenth of the income and own a mere one-hundredth of the property. In one study, the International Labour Organization (ILO) identified seventeen different agricultural tasks and determined that, in Africa, women did fourteen of them.

The inequalities that pervade the lives of the poverty-stricken and create hunger are very apparent. It's pervasive in these countries. It is very sad and very difficult to be black, a woman, or a female child in some places on this planet.

When we were in Africa, I saw one pretty little black girl who was pregnant. I found out she was twelve-years-old. She had one baby tied to her back in a sling. I learned that when their wives die, and so many of them do die young, the men take new wives from among the young girls. Girls are often sold by their parents.

But the boys and girls just capture my heart when we go into these countries to deliver food. I find them always to be so polite. I found myself hugging and loving them. I wanted to embrace them all. . .there were so many. I hoped they sensed how much I love them. I told them through an interpreter that I was giving them your love too—the love of Christians from around the world.

"Let the Little Children Come to Me"

Jesus said it. How can we ignore it? "Let the little

children come to Me. . .for of such is the kingdom of heaven" (Matthew 19:14 NKJ).

Just prior to this, He had told His disciples they were to be like little children (see Matthew 18:3). Twice, within a short period of time, Jesus drew these precious little ones to His bosom declaring their infinite worth both in His actions and in His words. Kingdom entrance, He declared, won't happen until and unless we take upon ourselves the beautiful attributes of little children.

Jesus Focused on the Worth of Little Children

Jesus focused on the worth of little children and we'd better pay attention. To allow these little ones to suffer and die because of food deprivation must be, in the eyes of the Father, an enormous injustice.

Oh, how much we need to value children! Don't allow the literature to somehow devalue them in your thinking. A brochure or an ad in a magazine may say, "It doesn't cost much to sponsor a child," or " For a few cents a day. . .," these may be facts that are quite true, but what is of major importance is the truth that an investment in saving the lives of children is an investment for time and eternity. Our pennies and our dollars count, but we don't just tip, as it were, to appease the God of the Good Book.

These vulnerable hungry little ones with the dark circles under their eyes, dressed in rags, are little jewels that can sparkle for Jesus if given even half a chance. I want you to see them for who they actually are.

In the days of His flesh here upon earth, Jesus was no mystic as He walked and talked among men. He spoke of familiar things and entered into everyday experiences of those with whom He mingled. In so doing, He made them sacred for ever. Therefore, to recognize fully what Jesus was doing in not only verbally acknowledging the presence and the worth of these children, but in demonstrating His love for them, is to grasp the importance of giving more than lip service ourselves.

Jesus is our example. To do anything less than to extend ourselves on behalf of children is to fall short of doing what Jesus said we were to do. The value and potential of children are constantly enforced in the Bible. Child by child communities and countries are created.

Known to Their Creator

Millions of infants and children have died from the effects of hunger and food deprivation. Unknown by name to us, each was known to their Creator. They were precious to Him.

The Bible often speaks about children. From its opening pages to the end, the terms, "child" and "children" occur almost two thousand times. The Bible children were real boys and girls like those in the world today. Sorrowful stories of lust, dishonor and the suffering of innocent children appear on its pages. We read, for instance, of wicked King Ahaz "who made his son pass through the fire [and offered him as a sacrifice] in accord with the abominable [idolatrous] practices of the [heathen] nations. . ." (2 Kings 16:3 AMP).

The prophets Hosea and Amos speak of infants being dashed to pieces, and of pregnant women being ripped open (Hosea 13:16; Amos 1:13). (See also Nahum 3:10.)

We read of the suffering of the children of Israel

(meaning the people, but certainly including infants and small children), and how God responded to that.

We know that God didn't allow Hagar, Sarah's maid, who was with child by Abraham, to starve or die from lack of water in the wilderness (see Genesis 16). God saw that unborn child in the mother's womb and His mercy reached out to her.

When Joshua and Caleb were sent by Moses to spy out the land, and the people murmured and complained because of their report, God was displeased. He spoke judgment against those who murmured and they did not get into the promised land. "But your little ones," God said, "whom you said would be victims, I will bring in, and they shall know the land which you have despised" (Numbers 14:31 NKJ).

One reads with horror the historical accounts of barbarous heathen times where the life of sick or deformed children was not thought worth preserving. Sickly children were thrown out as not worth saving. It was Christianity that brought about a change in attitude toward children. Godly adults adopted sick and unwanted children. Christian institutions and hospitals came into being where these little ones could receive love and help, and be given hope.

Oh, how much children today need the life-giving loving touch of humans acting on behalf of the Savior! To walk through those refugee camps and to see the way those children live is just to feel sick inside. How we want to help them! We long to do for them what they are incapable of doing for themselves.

Human nature hasn't changed much since the ancient Scriptures were written. The sword of the Chaldeans fell upon the city of Jerusalem with sons and daughters falling; famine and pestilence claimed hundreds of thousands of others; the wrath of a jealous, paranoid king was felt in Bethlehem and the mothers all but drowned in their sorrow (Matthew 2:16-18).

Whether by the sword or death from starvation, God is angry when innocent infants and children are the victims.

Famine's Faces

U.S. News & World Report (February 6, 1989) with bold headlines declared: **STARVATION AS A POLITICAL WEAPON.** The subhead reads: "Famine in Sudan, caused by government action, may be worse than in Ethiopia, 1984."

It is a story we had been tracking for many months as we endeavored to find a way to reach these starving Sudanese. The article speaks of a special compound housing Sudanese orphans driven mad by the horrors of losing their families to civil war and starvation. "Some have gone mad, baying and whimpering like stray dogs. These are kept in a special compound, bound hand and foot with string and vines."

It shows how doctors struggle to save malaria-stricken children. "Sudan's war takes its heaviest toll in small victims."

It speaks of famine's faces, referring to hungry refugee children wearing doctor's feeding instructions on tags around their necks as they wait for a meager camp meal.

The article appeared right at the time our food shipments had arrived at a seaport city ready to be transported via truck or train into the midst of this mass of human suffering. I read of the children writhing naked in the dust, their eyes pleading silently out of skeletal heads, bloody sores covering matchstick legs. I looked at the pictures and the words describing their little emaciated bodies racked with malaria and other diseases.

Staff of Life

In the photo story, I see a rat being held by its tail between the skeletal legs of two boys. The caption reads: Meat for sale. Boys trap rats for food.

Rats, at 25 cents apiece, and lily pods were the only food for sale in a market at a refugee camp.

Religious Warfare

Overland supplies of food had been cut off for months with the rebels attacking food convoys and shooting down relief planes. Western relief organizations had been expelled from the country. Even offers by some charity groups to send relief supplies to both government and rebel-held areas, had been denied. Clearly, starvation as a political weapon was the motive for starving a quarter-million people. It is religious warfare.

Hunger is the last battleground with Islamic fundamentalists in control. What they cannot gain militarily, they hope to win through famine.

Assault on the Stomach

This is what famine and hunger is all about. The assault on the stomach in most cases is successful. Millions wander hopelessly from town to town searching for food. The *U.S. News & World Report* feature sums it up all to clearly: "As with all famines, the children suffer most. In the town of Abyei, not a single child under 2½ years of age has survived the season of hunger."

The majority of these Sudanese victims fleeing war and famine have been Christians. A whole group of tribespeople face the very real possibility of extinction. Males are regarded as potential enemies. A scorched-earth policy has prevailed with the military pillaging and burning villages. Well-fed soldiers beat refugees standing in food lines and gleefully watch them starve.

I have seen Jesus in the eyes of hungry children. The words of Matthew 25 ring true.

This passage tells us that when the Son of Man comes in His glory, all the nations will be gathered before Him, and He will separate them one from another, as a shepherd divides his sheep from the goats. The sheep will be on His right hand, the goats on the left.

> Then the King will say. . ."Come, you blessed of my Father, inherit the kingdom prepared for you. . .for I was hungry and you gave me food. . ." Then the righteous will answer Him, saying, "Lord, when did we see You hungry and feed You. . .?" And the King will answer and say to them, "Assuredly, I say to you, inasmuch as you did it to one of the least of these My brethren, you did it to Me" (Matthew 25:34-35a, 40 NKJ).

These are the words of a King spoken about people whom He will separate upon the basis of character. What an hour of separation that will be!

The reward of the King to those on His right hand will be blessing and inheritance of the Kingdom of God. Admittance will be on the basis of their attitude to Christ as revealed in their attitude toward His people on earth.

Jesus is talking here about loyalty to the will of God. You cannot be against the ideals and the character of the Kingdom and hope to gain favor and blessing from the King and entrance into the benefits of His Kingdom. It's that simple. The message is plain.

Jesus is saying, "By your neglect of the hungry and needy of the earth, you have neglected Me." These are solemn words. Oh, how much we need to hear them in our hearts and respond now.

Millions are dying of hunger, including precious, innocent infants and children. We are ready to go into these hunger pockets of the world. You can be the arms and hands of God's people to help feed the hungry. The King has given a mandate. Will you be among the sheep or the goats?

A Cry to the Youth of the World

I cry out to the youth of the world to hear the truth regarding the children and youth of the world. In times of tragedy, youth often bear the brunt of it and are hurt the most.

I would like to enlist the youth of the Christian world to assist me in combating world hunger. I address you with deepest sincerity, LeSEA's End-Time Joseph program is not a game, it is not a sideline, but with deepest conviction, we say that especially among the youth of the Third World countries, we do not want them to die of starvation.

68

We need your energy and your vision to help in rescuing them.

Young men and women, I call upon you to help attack the problems contributing to world hunger. From all world news, hunger is rising like a specter to destroy. For sure, hunger is the dark hole of death. This is especially true of the children and youth of Third World countries.

I believe there are multitudes of Christian youth who are now ready to combat world hunger. We can do it together.

Needed: End-Time Josephs for the End Times

In Jerusalem, the Lord spoke to me in the nighttime saying that world hunger is a prophetic situation. The Bible says that in the last part of this dispensation there shall be great famines worldwide. God said that the End-Time Joseph Program was to collect and preserve mountains of food especially to feed the believers of the world during this most difficult time. As Joseph was the answer in Egypt in their days of distress, the End-Time Joseph Program can be the answer in these end-time days. We must never forget that although Joseph prophesied there would be good years and there would be years of famine, he also prepared for the bad years and had the answer when famine and hunger came.

God is speaking to Christian youth, telling them to combat world hunger before the return to earth of Jesus of Nazareth as King of kings and Lord of lords.

Youth of the Christian world, hear my plea. Feel my intensity and let's do it together!

7 Hunger's Effects

No other disaster compares with the outrage of world hunger.

Have you ever wondered what happened to the still-surviving but starving survivors in the German horror camps upon their liberation at the end of World War II? What actually does happen to the body when it is deprived of food?

We've all seen pictures of these emaciated prisoners of war, their deep-sunken eyes peering out from their gaunt faces. They were nothing but tightly stretched skin over bones. I read of the infamous concentration camp of Bergen-Belsen located 55 miles south of Hamburg, Germany. When the victorious British Army reached the camp on April 12, 1945, they found fifty-five thousand barely surviving inmates, many of them near death.

Medical experts armed with special food and equipment were flown in to save as many of these camp victims as possible. But thousands were dying. Hospital accommodations were improvised and the patients were treated one by one. Predigested proteins were given by intravenous injection, but it worsened their condition. Then they tried giving these vital nutrients by mouth, but they were found to be unpalatable. The reaction of the patients was one of undisguised horror.

They had been treated so savagely by their Nazi captors, and now they were still dying even with these well-meant efforts to save them. Not one of these experts had foreseen what would work best for these victims of starvation. But then it was discovered that the best treatment was to feed them skimmed milk by mouth. That is why even today, when you see pictures of food being unloaded, often you will observe these vast containers of powdered milk. That is why we are so happy when we are able to obtain powdered milk and we can get it into these needy places.

Millions have died from starvation, but health professionals have not always known the best way to resuscitate people who are near death from this cause. There has actually been an appalling dearth of information on the subject.

Malnutrition the Culprit

Lowered resistance to disease caused by malnutrition is the primary cause of death for those who have been food deprived. It's not too hard to understand. When famine strikes, or a person is deprived of food for whatever reason, the reduced intake of food is going to lower the body's resistance.

It's not only famine conditions, but what is termed "undernutrition" defined as deficient bodily nutrition due to inadequate food intake or faulty assimilation resulting in the walking skeletons you see in pictures.

Malnutrition refers to poor nutritional status arising from deficiencies of specific nutrients or from diets based on the wrong kinds or wrong proportions of food. This insufficient intake of energy and protein combined with poor biological utilization is the most serious type of malnutrition.

And always compounding the precarious food situation problem in refugee camps, famine or war-devastated areas, is the unavailability of health services. An outbreak of measles, for instance, could sweep through the camp, and without nourishment the bodies of little children have no resistance, there is nothing to fight with, and they become statistics.

Malnutrition is usually associated with poverty, poor sanitation, and lack of primary health care. I recall reading a number of years ago something Dr. Stanley Mooneyham said about malnutrition: "Malnutrition induced by war's displacement may not be as spectacular as an exploding rocket, but it can be just as deadly."

Conventional diseases always increase in incidence and severity when there is food deprivation. One of the reasons it is so hard to get an accurate handle on deaths resulting from starvation is because rarely will death be attributed to starvation. Officials of a country and public reaction is such that they will seek to avoid the stigma of the label starvation for a country or a region. I have learned that famine watchers worldwide actually measure the severity of a food situation by the increase in the death rate attributed to conventional diseases.[1]

Social Injustice

When a population has to adjust to a short food supply, first to die usually are the ill, the aged, the very young, and then the poor. Those who survive the best are the wealthy and the strong. The hungry, for the most part, have one thing in common—they are all poor. Usually it is poverty that starves people to death, not necessarily the callous whims of nature, nor even the stupidity of war. Economics has a lot to do with who goes hungry and who survives. People die because they are poor and cannot afford to buy whatever food is available. They are powerless at the hands of the powerful. It is called social injustice.

For instance, anemias are a complex group of diseases in which the oxygen-carrying, circulating red blood cells are deficient in quality or quantity or both. Perhaps you have heard someone say, "He has iron-deficient anemia," meaning his body is not getting enough iron. The red substance of the red blood cells is the protein hemoglobin. That is where most of the iron in the body is found. But a person should not have to die just because he is anemic.

Ecology in the Womb

Tragically, even though many lives may be saved as a result of food reaching them in time, the damage that has been done to the developing brains of babies in the womb, or to little children. . ., I repeat, the prenatal damage is just incalculable.

This hemoglobin in the red blood cells, as I understand it, is essential to the transporting of oxygen from the lungs to every part of the body. Consider this, muscles can store oxygen, but the brain is unable to do so. Therefore, the brain is critically dependent on a sustained oxygen supply. So iron plays many crucial roles in the well-being of the body. Deprive the body of the nutrients that supply iron (and other vital nutrients), and you begin to get a picture of the devastating effects of hunger.

An infant with a full-sized brain could not be delivered through the female birth canal, so God has created us in such a way that the brain nearly triples in size during the first year of life. Isn't that amazing? But for this rapid postnatal growth of the brain to take place, it requires a sustained supply of appropriate nutrients in adequate quantity. If that doesn't happen, normal brain development is seriously jeopardized.

Now if you find that as interesting as I do, what is even more spectacular is the prenatal period of growth. The psalmist knew what he was talking about when he refers to God knowing him in his mother's womb. "You have formed my inward parts," David wrote, "You have covered me in my mother's womb. I will praise You, for I am fearfully and wonderfully made" (Psalm 139:13-14 NKJ).

But during those nine months of gestation a process is going on precisely programmed by the Master-Creator. No complex architectural edifice begins to compare. However, raw materials called food are needed to help get the job done right. Any failure in logistics during that time can be fatal to the brain structure taking place. A chronic deficiency of resources such as caused by malnutrition cannot always be reversed, and a brain-defective human will be born.

Now that's a very simple explanation, I know, but the point to remember is that prenatal malnutrition can seriously affect a person's entire life by severly inhibiting the number of neurons produced before birth. I look at our grandchildren—healthy, intelligent, beautiful little girls and boys—and I thank God daily that they weren't carried in the wombs of women deprived of life-sustaining food.

In 1987, 87,000,000 babies were born worldwide. Our accountant figured that this would translate into approximately three new babies being born every second (the actual figure comes out to be 2.75). When you consider how many of those babies are born in Third World countries and in places where war, famine, and man's inhumanity to man, take place, you begin to form in your mind's eye a clearer picture of this monster called hunger with all its ill effects.

The damage done to humans by rebellion and war throughout recorded history is well-documented. Furthermore, we have some idea of what happens in places where natural disasters occur—drought-ravaged Sudan, for instance, the floods, the locusts, earthquakes, cyclones, hurricanes, typhoons. But what is beginning to emerge in more recent times is the effects of starvation brought about by man-made plagues—depriving people of food, governments deliberately and cynically starving people to death just to improve their bargaining position. The horror stories are so terrible it's just hard to believe people could be so cruel.

Long-Lasting Effects

Worldwide we know there are pockets of hunger where malnourished mothers are not contributing adequately to normal placental development so that fetal growth is affected. And this has been going on for many years. What kind of children are they bringing into the world? What is going to happen to those who survive in the years ahead?

Because it isn't possible to experiment with pregnant women to determine placental adequacy, modern medicine and biology relies on animal studies. While the animal right's protestors demonstrate, the validity of what this research produces has become the cornerstone for almost all advances reported by research teams. We know that depriving pregnant rats of protein results in a reduced number of brain cells in their offspring. As they mature, these rats manifest many abnormalities. It is safe to say that in many places throughout the world today, whole generations of humans will grow up mentally retarded or with major brain defects, deafness, blindness and physically handicapped or disabled in other ways, if they even survive. It will be traceable to food deprivation.

These children will never reach their full biological potential, either physical or mental, no matter how well they are fed in later years. You cannot walk through these refugee camps and observe these children and adults without recognizing that we are already seeing this. Dietary deficiencies result in the stunting of the body as a whole.

Not only do these children bring a deficient mind to the

task of growing up, they are condemned to do poorly in school, with all the consequences this may bring upon him, his family, and society at large. It is a vicious cycle. A fulfilled life? What do you think?

And now researchers are telling us that the influence of malnutrition, including mental retardation, may extend well beyond the malnourished parents and their offspring to the second generation, even if that second generation is well fed.

The Meaning of Words

The words themselves used when we speak of world hunger are used interchangeably, but they can actually mean different things. I have already introduced you to the words "malnutrition" and "undernutrition." More than anything, I wanted you to see that 80 percent of total brain development takes place between the moment of conception and the age of two, and that medical science is in agreement that severe malnutrition produces irreversible brain damage. Malnutrition is producing millions of retarded children worldwide.

I do not believe we have begun to realize the long-lasting effects and problems that world hunger has and is going to create. Neither do I believe the world is prepared to cope with what they will find they have on their hands in the years to come.

So let me define a few more words for you. "Hunger" itself is the group of symptoms that arise from the depletion of food in the body. But these symptoms can disappear quite quickly when food is received.

"Malnutrition," relates to the impairment or risk of impairment to mental and physical health resulting from the failure to meet the total nutrient requirements of an individual.

"Starvation" is considered the most extreme form of malnutrition. Accompanying starvation are the physiological symptoms you see in pictures—the edema (swelling of tissue), and often severe and sustained diarrhea which is the frequent prelude to death. Adults can survive starvation if it isn't too prolonged; they have bodily reserves they can draw upon for a time. Actually, a healthy human being can go without food for six weeks, as we know from hunger strikes. If, however, hard physical effort or constrained labor is forced upon a starving person, they are reduced to living skeletons and will be unable to carry out the simplest physical and mental tasks. This is what made it so difficult for the prisoners of war in the Nazi concentration camps.

Mature adults will usually recover from near starvation, but young, growing children will not. That is why we say children are the most vulnerable victims. The price being paid in unrelenting misery and human degradation is something I hope this chapter has been able to help you see.

The first manifestation of hunger is the gnawing desire for food, accompanied by surliness, aggression and frenzied activity With the passage of time if food is not supplied, energy diminishes, strength wanes, and activity is reduced. Before death there comes lassitude, listlessness, weakness and exhaustion. Thus, toward the end, nature eases the ordeal.[2]

The consequences of the human destruction caused by

hunger, malnutrition and starvation, are greater than those of all wars and epidemics put together.

The number of people who die as a direct result of malnutrition is equivalent to dropping a Hiroshima bomb every three days.

No wonder Jesus told us to feed the hungry.

---

1. Don Paarlberg, *Toward a Well-Fed World* (Ames, Iowa: Iowa State University Press, 1988), p. 4.

2. Ibid.

8 The Paradox: Hunger in the Midst of Plenty

Hunger is an outrage precisely because it is profoundly needless.[1]

In 1974 the first World Food Conference convened in Rome and created the UN World Food Council to monitor and coordinate implementation of more than twenty recommendations for the production, distribution and consumption of food for food-deficit countries. Strategies were designed that included helping to activate the untapped productivity of the world's small farmers, most of whom, especially in Africa, are women. Ways were recommended to enlist the participation of poor people themselves in the decisions that profoundly affect their lives. And yet, here we are these many years later, and we still find oursleves confronting the problem of hunger in a world of abundant harvests.

It is a tragic paradox—hunger in the midst of plenty. The dark hole of death.

What conclusions can be reached? I would like you to understand that hunger is not simply the result of adverse weather, nor is it simply a failure to produce adequate food supplies. Those are myths. They need to be debunked.

Hunger, Poverty and Powerlessness

Hunger exists largely as the result of policies and actions that are insensitive to the poor. Much of the time the situation—even in a country like America where the problem of the homeless and the hungry is beginning to surface like it never has before, much to the embarrassment of our politicians—I repeat, much of the time the hopelessness of a situation and the unwillingness of society to do the right things means that the victims live in a constant state of deprivation and poverty.

Research is consistently revealing that it is generally accepted that hunger is caused by poverty and poverty is caused by powerlessness. Some researchers think that people are hungry because they are poor, and they are poor because they don't have the power to choose to be otherwise.[2] I have found that most often poverty is related strongly to transgression of God's laws.

Material advantages invariably fall into the hands of the powerful, and what the poor lack, as much as anything else, is the power to secure what they really need. Among other things, the diseases of poverty weaken people so much that they are very often physically unable to do what needs to be done to try and improve their lot in life.

Uninformed people often accuse the poor of being lazy and indolent. They say things like: "Well, they neet to get out there and work, raise themselves by their bootstraps and do something." Some of them do not even have boots!

As to the accusation that they are lazy, if the truth were known, most of the time the poor are so ill-fed as to be greatly weakened by malnutrition or undernutrition. It isn't laziness; it's poor physical health producing a lethargy and inability to exert themselves.

Blanket generalizations are very unwise. Certainly there are lazy people in the world. I have met them; so have you. And usually they are poor, though not necessarily starving. Somehow they have managed to get on the welfare system and food stamps and they are not suffering. So when I say the poor and powerless, I am not referring to those who have taken advantage of a system meant to help the truly poor. But if you had seen poverty and the desperately poor as I have in so many countries, then you would agree that being poor and powerless is a real problem for millions of people in a world of plenty.

The Bible Has Much to Say About the Poor

More than anything, what it reveals to me is the all-too-obvious fact that we are a world insensitive to the plight of the poor; we have not obeyed the Bible's instructions regarding caring for the needy and the hungry. Jesus Himself said the poor would always be with us (Matthew 26:11; John 12:3-8).[3] The Gospels show Jesus' love and concern for the poor wherever He went.

At the age of seventeen, Lester Sumrall was miraculously healed of tuberculosis. Three weeks later he announced to his parents that he was leaving home to preach the gospel.

During the early 1930s, Lester joined Howard Carter on a missionary journey that lasted two and a half years. Here he is riding in a mule train traveling through the mountains of Tibet. The two men ministered in China, Japan, Manchuria, and Tibet, then through Russia on the Trans-Siberian railroad, and from there into pre-war Europe.

Lester Sumrall on the back of a pick-up truck in Zimbabwe shares the powerful message of the resurrected Christ who brings life to all who call on Him.

A group of children eagerly surround Dr. Sumrall after recent food distribution program in Zimbabwe, Africa.

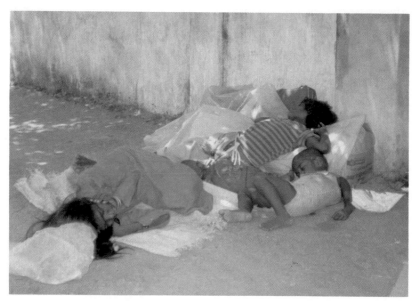

This picture was taken in Sri Lanka, but it is becoming a common scene in many cities of the world. Hungry people without a home!

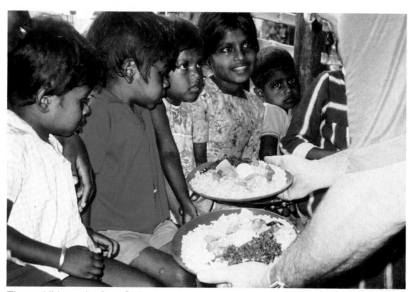

These children, also from Sri Lanka, are being served a nutritious meal. Feed the Hungry has been involved in this ongoing feeding program since 1986.

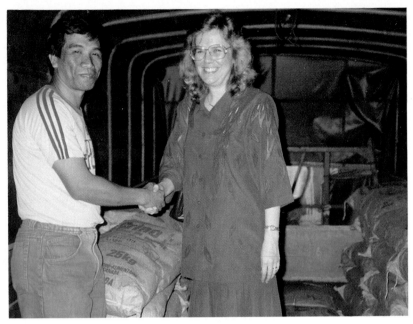

Beverly Sumrall from Bethel Temple in Manila, Philippines gives sacks of powdered milk to a local pastor. The milk was sent by Feed the Hungry.

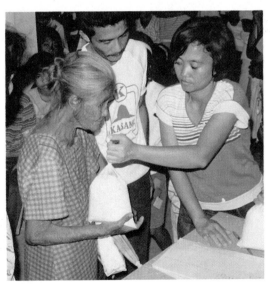

The pastor from the church above had the milk distributed among needy people of his congregation.

The face of gratitude. This little Costa Rican boy is thankful that someone sent food when he was hungry.

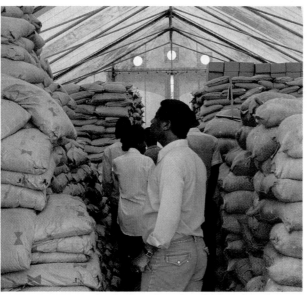

Temporary storage for food ready to be distributed in the Sudanese refugee camp in Ethiopia.

After the typhoons and flooding, hundreds of thousands of people were left homeless in Bangladesh. They resorted to building makeshift shelters of scraps of material left by the storms.

Dr. Sumrall and Ulf Ekman, international director from Sweden, joined Pastor Swapon Bose, founder of the Bangladesh Free Baptist churches at their annual conference. Feed the Hungry helped procure food to be distributed by forty pastors who attended the daily pastors' seminars.

Lester Sumrall and Howard Carter visited a Bible school in Poland during their missionary journey in the 1930s.

Poland revisited. Dr. Sumrall and a team of pastors ministered and delivered 89.2 tons of food. From L to R: Paul Forsen, Robert Ekh, Carl Gustaf Severin from Sweden, Tennyson and Carol Fitch, Lester Sumrall, Rudy Vrtachnik, United States, Oliver Lindberg, Sweden, and Harley Kolterman, United States. As with all our feeding outreaches, we work directly with local pastors and churches assuring us that the food reaches the needy in their villages and communities.

HUNGER IN THE BIG APPLE

Walking through the inner city of New York, Lester Sumrall joins Bill Wilson, pastor of Metro Church, in viewing the great need of New York City. The streets were filled with litter, trashed autos and discarded appliances. This is the playground of the city children.

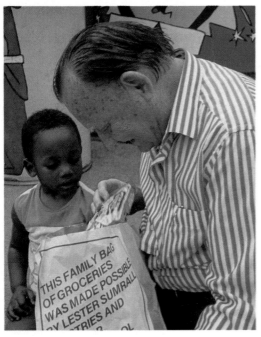

Dr. Sumrall hands a bag of groceries to a boy attending a special program for inner-city children called "Yogi Bear Sidewalk Sunday School." In contrast to starving children viewed in other photos, the children of the inner cities look healthy but are often suffering from malnutrition.

Ellen Parsley is World Director of Queen's Court, the women's division of Feed-the-Hungry. She fell in love with the children at Metro Church in New York City. These children are hungry for love as well as food.

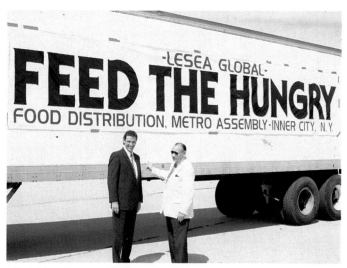

Rod Parsley and Lester Sumrall in front of the semi-truck loaded with food bound for the ghettos of New York City. Feed the Hungry also supports the Metro Church ministry among children on a monthly basis.

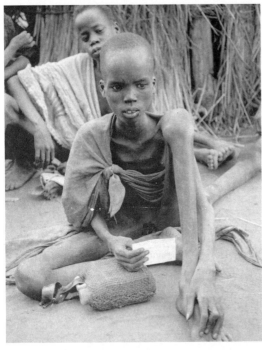

Look at the despair and hopelessness written on the faces of these boys. They fled from Sudan to Ethiopia looking for help. We must not fail them.

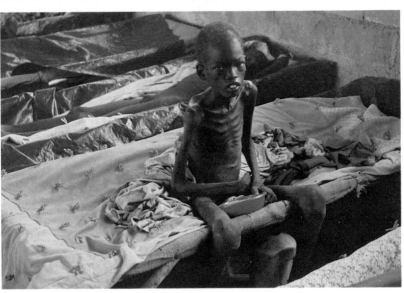

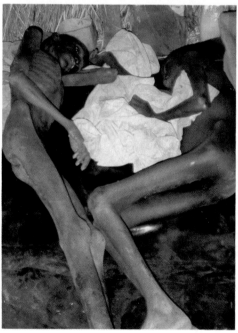

One white face in a sea of black faces. It is Robert Ekh from Sweden who came to deliver food, powdered milk and Bibles from Feed the Hungry.

In the picture to the left we no doubt have come too late. Their bodies are just bones. Could they possibly survive?

Furnaces of the Nazi death camps where millions of Jews were exterminated during World War II.

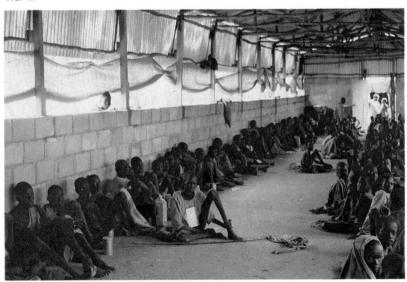

These starving people in an Ethiopian refugee camp make you think of the people in the Nazi death camps. Most of the refugees are from Sudan, victims of a cruel war. They are fleeing for their lives, and are in desperate need of food, water, clothing and medical attention.

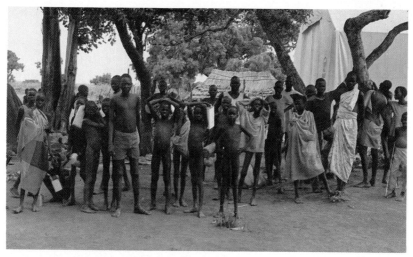

Many of the refugees are young boys who managed to escape. The enemy killed their fathers and raped their mothers and sisters before taking them into slavery. Some of the children lost their minds as a result of the horrible things they have experienced.

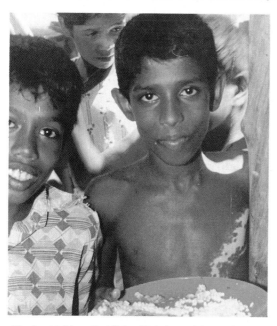

The Lord told me that if the Christians of the world would fast breakfast and lunch every Friday and give the money they saved to feed those who are hungry, we could help bring an end to the suffering of many hungry people around the world.

95

This is a refugee village in Costa Rica. People who have fled their homes in Nicaragua because of the war may have to live like this for years. The main desire of those to whom we spoke was that God's people pray for their families, their friends and their country.

Surrounded by Russian pastors, many who had come from great distances, Dr. Sumrall explained The End-Time Joseph Program, and how it is his prayerful hope that Feed the Hungry will be able to help meet the hunger needs in Armenia and other places in Russia where the people are suffering. "I have never found more desire and hunger for the word of God than we encountered in Russia," Dr. Sumrall reported.

The End-Time Joseph Program to Feed-the-Hungry is a three-pronged outreach: 1. Food distribution; 2.Pastors' seminars; 3. Evangelism, healing and delivering the oppressed. This picture was taken in Costa Rica where Dr. Sumrall and pastors Jim Andrews and Robyn Gool ministered to those in need.

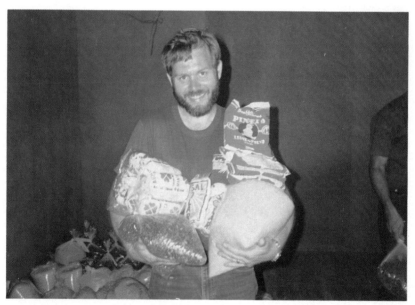

Pastor Tennyson Fitch from Indiana shows samples of food which will be given to the refugees in Costa Rica. Thank you for helping make this possible!

Dr. Lester Sumrall is the senior pastor of Christian Center Cathedral of Praise in South Bend, Indiana. This is also the world headquarters of LeSEA Ministries, which includes The End-Time Joseph Program to Feed the Hungry. LeSEA is a multifaceted outreach which includes television stations, a radio station, and shortwave radio reaching around the world to win precious souls to Jesus.

A view from the dome auditorium seating 3,500. Around the walls hang the flags of a hundred nations to remind us of our global mission of reaching the millions yet untold.

In many places throughout both the Old and New Testaments, we are reminded of the need to look after the poor. Apparently the disciples never forgot what Jesus said about looking after the poor, and this was passed on to the Apostle Paul (see Galatians 2:10). Paul carried with him a great concern for the poor and needy. He took offerings for them. He identified with them, considering himself to be one with them in their homelessness, their hunger, being thirsty, and being poorly clothed.

> To this very hour we go hungry and thirsty, we are in rags, we are brutally treated, we are homeless (1 Corinthians 4:14 NIV).

James, believed to be the half-brother of Jesus, and the recognized leader of the Jerusalem church,[4] in his New Testament letter, has a great deal to say about treating the poor with equality (James 2:2-13). We are to be merciful people. "What good is it, my brothers, if a man claims to have faith but has no deeds? Can such faith save him? Suppose a brother or sister is without clothes and daily food. If one of you says to him, 'Good, I wish you well; keep warm and well fed,' but does nothing about his physical needs, what good is it? In the same way, faith by itself, if it is not accompanied by action, is dead" (James 2:14-17 NIV).

In the Old Testament we hear David lamenting the lot of the poor in many of the Psalms. The "oppression of the poor" and "the sighing of the needy," he says, are known to God (Psalm 12). In 37 places the psalmist speaks of the poor. The promise is that "the needy shall not always be forgotten;" the expectation of the poor shall not perish forever (Psalm 9:18).

The Proverbs speak of the poor with great sensitivity. Solomon infers that the poor may have more understanding than the rich (Proverbs 28:11). "Better is the poor who walks in his integrity than one perverse in his ways, though he be rich" (Proverbs 28:6; see also Proverbs 19:1).

There are many cautions given about how to regard and treat the poor and needy. We would be wise to become familiar with them and to heed them. We will be held accountable for how we have treated them. "He who has pity on the poor lends to the Lord, And He will pay back what he has given" (Proverbs 19:17 NKJ).

"The righteous considers the cause of the poor, But the wicked does not understand such knowledge" (Proverbs 29:7 NKJ).

The World's Treatment of the Poor

One of my associates attended the 1988 World Food Conference held in Des Moines, Iowa. It was the first time in more than a decade that world leaders had gathered to address world food policy issues. She was one of five hundred conveners from 22 nations that included Iowa State and other university participants, in addition to guests representing the governments of different countries, including the U.S. Many private interest groups, associations and organizations were present including such companies as Dow Chemical, seed companies, the American Soybean Association, and others. Farm groups were represented with farmer speaker representatives in abundance. Private doner organizations (called PDOs) were there including Church World Service, Catholic Relief Services, Luthern

World Relief, American Jewish Joint Distribution Committee, Heifer Project International, the Self-Help Foundation, and our own organization, LeSEA.

There was much rhetoric and speeches about trade policies, trade reform, legislative perspectives, credit availability, economic reform, etc. But one astute gentleman from the European Parliament captured her attention and received applause when he stood up urging that more consideration be given to people than these other subjects.

In spite of that man's statement, the focus constantly turned toward economic and agricultural policies. There was a great deal of concern being expressed by the farm associations and their farmer members about the need for continued farm subsidies, and she saw a lot of private lobbying efforts going on in the lobby and halls as legislators were being cornered.

A man from the Netherlands kept pointing out in different sessions that the hunger problem worldwide is basically a poverty problem. Later, in a private conversation with this man, they agreed that if the hungry could eat words, Africa and other desperately needy areas of the world, would have recovered as a result of the ongoing rhetoric.

However, there were helpful and informative things being said, and spokespeople for the poor did have opportunity to speak their hearts. The Hollander emphasized forcefully that the poor are outside the marketing-oriented problems that were being discussed at such length. "They have no part in policy-making," he said. "It is not enough just to look at agriculture or trade issues. We must take an overall look before we come up with judgments. The poor receive little benefit from much talk about policies to eradicate hunger."

Such views weren't necessarily popular with the majority of the people present, it seemed, many of whom represented private industry and farming interests—people who would benefit from policy-oriented discussions and recommendations. Advocates for the poor insisted that a closer look at cooperative policies between rich and poor countries would provide more opportunity to eradicate poverty, that resource constraints of the poor countries are a problem of tremendous magnitude. "Income distribution is a major problem," one gentlemen pointed out. "More 'free trade' in agriculture is not necessarily a good thing. Developing countries are stuck with vast numbers of unemployed people which creates a monumental problem in the poverty picture. Trade liberalization will not necessarily help the poor."

It was good to know that there are people in the world who do recognize the poverty picture. A man from India pointed out that countries not considered "poor" should not be so arrogant as to think they have all the answers. "You demean nations too often in your aid efforts," he said. "Self-interest motivates many people. But our people need tools to work with; they need roads so they can get their crops to market. They have health problems. It's hard for people to be effective when they are battling with malaria for instance."

Debt management is a major problem for Third World countries.

The need for economic reform is a valid need, but the problem of multi-national companies pushing poor people off their land in Third World countries was of major concern. Many of these are government-sanctioned monopolies who are developing a tremendous power base, literally raping the country's resources, depriving the nationals of the means to support their families.

It was pointed out that many powerful people in these countries are benefiting from subsidies; not the poor people for whom subsidies are intended. It was pointed out, for instance, that the economic policies of the Marcos regime in the Philippines inhibited growth and economic reform. The people did not benefit from this.

The Poverty Trap

That people get trapped in poverty can never be denied, not by any thinking person. Hunger is an overwhelming, endemic problem in developing world countries. The great majority of the world's hungriest people, actually an estimated 90 percent according to the World Bank, live and work in rural areas, a long way from the main centers of wealth. Many of these people are tenant farmers or landless labourers. If they do own land, it would be just a very small plot.

Poor farmers do not have advantages afforded to the more affluent. For instance, they lack access to credit and to technical support that could improve production of their meager crops.

The cities in these developing world countries are swelling rapidly as people are forced off the land and migrate to the cities. There they are once again confronted with the reality of the inequalities of life—the unequal distribution of purchasing power, the difficulties they encounter in finding employment.

The circumstances in which the poor live are as varied as the many cultures of the human race; but the one thing they all share in common is that they are all poor and, for the most part, hungry. Many times there is food in the native villages, but it can be had only at the new price laid down by the government. If you do not have money to buy maize, or whatever the food staple is that would keep you and your family alive, what do you do?

Until it is widely acknowledged that the ongoing problems of world hunger are directly related to treatment of the poor, not much progress will be made in halting the growth of the problem. Until causes are examined in the institutions, policies and ideologies which widen the gap between the rich and poor, and until they are identified and changed, people will continue to suffer and die from hunger. It cannot be overemphasized that the poor are powerless within a system of injustice. The poverty trap is real.

Poverty is the basic cause of hunger. Hunger is one of the most visible parts of the problem. The causes of poverty are also the causes of hunger. What is needed is justice in a hungry world. Children, for instance, need to be educated. When you educate a child and give him an opportunity to fend for himself in the world, you break the cycle of family poverty.

The Christian Solution: The Time to Help is Now

There is a story in Luke's Gospel that I believe vividly

portrays for us the necessity to be about our Father's business today, now, while there is yet time. It is the story of the rich man and Lazarus, a diseased beggar, utterly destitute, reduced to begging alms, a man covered with ulcerated sores. One day someone laid Lazarus at the door of the rich man "who was splendidly clothed and lived each day in mirth and luxury." The account reads like this [as told by Jesus]:

> As he lay there longing for scraps from the rich man's table, the dogs would come and lick his open sores. Finally the beggar died and was carried by the angels to be with Abraham in the place of the righteous dead. The rich man also died and was buried, and his soul went into hell. There, in torment, he saw Lazarus in the far distance with Abraham.
>
> "Father Abraham," he shouted, "have some pity! Send Lazarus over here if only to dip the tip of his finger in water and cool my tongue, for I am in anguish in these flames."
>
> But Abraham said to him, "Son, remember that during your lifetime you had everything you wanted, and Lazarus had nothing. So now he is here being comforted and you are in anguish. And besides, there is a great chasm separating us, and anyone wanting to come to you from here is stopped at its edge; and no one over there can cross to us."
>
> Then the rich man said, "O Father Abraham, then please send him to my father's home—for I have five brothers— to warn them about this place of torment lest they come here when they die."
>
> But Abraham said, "The Scriptures have warned them again and again. Your brothers can read them any time they want to."
>
> The rich man replied, "No, Father Abraham, they won't

bother to read them. But if someone is sent to them from
the dead, then they will turn from their sins."

But Abraham said, "If they won't listen to Moses and the
prophets, they won't listen even though someone rises from
the dead."

— Luke 16:21-31 (TLB)

In every country there is "the rich man and a Lazarus."
Lazarus, while still alive, asked for only crumbs for his
dying body. The rich man who fared sumptuously on earth,
was reduced to begging for one drop of water in Hades.

While we feast and satisfy our gluttonous appetites, and
indulge our uncontrolled eating habits, more than 35,000
people die from hunger and starvation's related causes in
poverty-stricken areas of the world daily.

Compassion can end world hunger. The rich man had
no compassion for Lazarus. I pray to God that there will
be no rich Christians reading this who, after reading it,
will be able to remain indifferent to the plight of the world's
hungry people.

---

1. Frances Moore Lappe and Joseph Collins, *World Hunger* (New York, NY, Grove Press, Inc., 1986), p. 14.

2. From a 1987 *Report on the World Food Crisis, World Food Security: A Matter of Policy*, p. 6.

3. This should not be understood callously. Christ said, in effect, that there will be other opportunities to do good to the poor, but in the context of this setting, this occasion when He was talking to the disciples, He was saying they would not have many opportunities to do for Him what had just been done. (Mary had poured costly fragrant oil on Jesus, and the disciples had objected.)

4. Acts 12:17; 15:13; 21:8.

9 The World Hunger Belt and the Empires of History

Pagan decadence has contributed to the ongoing problem of world hunger.

In studying the major empires of history, I have discovered an amazing fact—the power belt historically of the nations lies in the middle of the world. Look at the drawing in Appendix C and you will see what I mean.

There have been six major empires in history which have ruled the world economically, artistically and intellectually. These empires are: Egypt, Assyria, Babylon, Persia, Greece and the Roman empires. What is interesting to note is that these empires are all located between the lines shown on the map, i.e., beginning at the top of the map, at the 60th parallel (the north), moving down to the Tropic of Cancer (on the south). It is this same area that has a con-

centration of major agricultural resources supplying much
of the food for the rest of the world. Many of the major
famines have occurred outside this belt.

The North-South Divide

The rich and poor countries can actually be shown as
having a North-South divide, with the countries of the
North (the First World) being mostly industrial market
economies. Non-market economies already comprise the
Second World, i.e., countries that are still the major con-
sumers of raw materials (food, minerals, oil, cotton) produced in the South. And nations of the South are referred
to as the Third World.

There is a term used by economists, governments and
those who study the world hunger problem. It's called
macroeconomics which refers to a study of economics in
terms of whole systems especially with reference to general
levels of output and income, and to how all this is inter-
related among various sectors of the economy.

It boils down to the haves and have nots. Victims are
not always in the poor countries. If that were the case, how
would you explain the bread lines and soup kitchens in the
United States? Ironic, isn't it? It's not food shortage
necessarily in many parts of the world, it is a shortage of
political morality that we face as we head into the twenty-
first century. If people go hungry in a world of plenty, it's
because someone somewhere is creating that hunger by
policies that discriminate against them.

At the level of macroeconomics, it is international trading systems—tariffs, commodity prices, quotas and

monopolies that are the culprits keeping poor countries at the mercy of the rich industrial world. Northern governments' policies on aid and military strategy have compounded the problems. There is no question in my mind but what economic policies pursued by wealthier nations undermine the development of poorer nations. It's a case of the pockets of the rich being lined far too often at the expense of the poor. Freedom from hunger is, among other things, a political issue, and a question of human rights. There is more than sufficient food currently being produced to feed every man, woman and child on planet Earth.

So it comes down to an unavoidable conclusion: What the poor and hungry lack more than anything is the power to secure what they really need. What is needed is more fair distribution of what is available, equal access to land, and the means to produce food (seeds, water and the means to irrigate if normal rains do not occur, some simple tools to aid the farmer in contrast to primitive means of tilling the land).

The Scandal of World Hunger

In this chapter I am only briefly exposing you to some of the issues behind the scandal of world hunger. It is a big subject. For instance, Brazil is considered now to be one of the richest nations in the world, yet there are an estimated 50 million people living there in extreme poverty, 40 million of whom are considered malnourished. Such enormous disparities in wealth exist on other continents such as Latin America, Africa and Asia.

And in the United States, though we do not like to admit

it, especially in our vast metropolitan areas, there are people living on the streets, roaming aimlessly seeking handouts, scavengers in garbage dumpsters, living in welfare hotels in the bleakest of surroundings. I think of Bill Wilson and the work he is doing in the ghettoes of New York City. We support this work and others like him in our country.[1]

Many of these people would be considered what is now being called "the new poor." They are people, some of whom were caught in the process of deindustrialization of our country when men and women were released from their manufacturing jobs. Now these breadwinners are without jobs and resources. Imagine that—hunger in a bountiful land such as ours. The roads out of poverty with its resultant hunger and other problems are roads difficult and sometimes impossible to find.

It is basically the world's system that determines who receives enough to eat. That's why the work of Christian relief organizations such as ours and others is so important. We seek to work within the perimeters established, not moving outside of that which is legal, but avoiding red tape and bureaucracy. We will not be intimidated into acquiescing to the demands of unfair systems. And because the needs are so great and we stand ready with desperately needed supplies, we find favor with governments and are able to move in with help and hope.

So it is an undeniable fact that northern countries which dominate the international economic system hold the balance of power.

Food Production

There are three main cereal crops that provide the basic food for most of the world (whether directly consumed or converted into meat and dairy products). They are wheat, rice and maize. Wheat production is dominated by the Soviet Union, the United States, and suprisingly, China. The United states also produces about 30 percent of the world's coarse grains, including maize (42 percent).[2]

The top five producers of rice, however, are all from the South with China leading the field (36 percent) and India second (19 percent). The success story of the "Green Revolution" in India is attributed to an American hunger fighter, Norman Borlaug, winner of the Nobel Peace Prize for his humanitarian efforts. I like what this man says as he talks about how he confronted the specter of world hunger. "A man has to be a torero, a bullfighter. He has to sidestep bureaucracy and red tape." This Green Revolution was and is primarily a phenomenon of high-yielding wheat and rice. While it began in Mexico with Borlaug, and spread throughout much of the world, it had its greatest impact in South Asia.

The success of the Green Revolution, however, is highly dependent on mechanization, fertilizer and high-energy imputs. These are things that are not available to millions of small landowners throughout the world. China, on the other hand, adopted sweeping political programs involving land reform, collectivized farming and what is really considered a remarkable health care system. So the Chinese depended on their single most valuable resource—human beings.

The creation of hunger in the Sudan and other places in Africa has its roots in many causes including, as I have already shown you in previous chapters, weather conditions and the drought, and mismanaged independence, civil strife, nation going to war against another nation in their own continent. But there are other forces that cannot be ignored. African elites have worsened the plight of their own countrymen through political and economic processes that set the scene for so much hardship. Someone has observed that whereas once it was slave ships, it is now planes, ships and telex machines that transfer Africa's wealth in the form of commodities and finance to the coffers of the North.

From Fortune to Famine

But isn't it amazing that a place like the Sudan was once considered the "bread-basket of the Arab world?" How does a nation go from stability to crisis? The answer is complex, but certainly control of her resources—human, mineral and agricultural—is one of the prime causes. The poor have no control. For these people, 87 percent of the population who live in the countryside, they have little, if any, contact with central government. The United Nations has estimated that at the height of the famine in the mid-1980s, 1.5 million Sudanese had been driven from their homes, 1 million were at risk of starvation, and an estimated 150 persons per day were dying of starvation.[3]

From fortunes to famine—the underlying theme is one of poverty, lack of land for the poor to farm, and systematic neglect. The people—victims of decisions to organize the national economy in specific ways that failed to take into account their future destiny.

The Tyranny of the New

There was a time when the traditional relationship

between landowners and tenants was mutually beneficial. Those who controlled the land knew that their tenant farmers produced their wealth. So they took care of them. They didn't starve.

With the advent of new methods of farming—mechanization, cash-cropping, and large-scale farming—changes came forcing the little people off the land. Traditional lifestyles of the peasant landowners that had existed for generations were suddenly gone. In its place came commercial farming geared towards the export market with those who did manage to maintain jobs increasingly vulnerable to the changing fortunes of the national economy.

This kind of exploitation of the small farmers and the nomads in many developing nations is an all-too-common tale. Investors and entrepreneurs who could afford it were able to wrest the land away from the people. Very often what remains is extreme wealth at one level and extreme poverty at another, with middlemen in between. But it is the landless rural poor and the jobless urban poor who suffer from increased poverty and hunger.

While progress brings some benefits, it also can be very disruptive. A common Sudanese expression is that most of the common people "will never taste the dollars."

Another Side to the Picture

There is yet another side to this picture of suffering and famine that is taking place in so many parts of the world. It is something not discussed by governments, economists, or by those who have purchasing power. It is something

I have long observed. The major heathen religions were born in the parts of the world that have experienced the greatest famines.

Look at the map in Appendix C again. Notice India. What is the dominant religion there? The answer is Hinduism. Notice China. Do most of the Chinese worship God? The Chinese religion is steeped in Confucianism, Taoism and Buddhism. The Japanese worship at the shrines of Shinto and Buddha. Eastern and central Asia are cultic devotees. Animism and demon worship are very strong in Africa.

When people turn their backs on God and worship pagan Gods, they weaken their nation and Satan takes control. These nations that have been and are in the throes of revolution, violence and death got there by allowing heathen religions to weaken them. The people die of starvation and disease.

If you believed that a cow was a god, you wouldn't eat the cow, you would go hungry. If you beleived that a flea or a tick was the reincarnation of one of your ancestors, you wouldn't kill it—you would suffer from the diseases it might carry. This is exactly the predicament of many people who follow after pagan religions today.

Scripture declares that in the last days more people will turn to heathen religions, idolatry and superstition (1 Timothy 4:1); it says that these things destroy a person's vital contact with God (Romans 11:22). A pagan is "cut off" from the God of life.

Turning One's Back on God Brings Consequences

When someone turns his back on God, he snaps the

anchor chain that would hold him steady in the storms of life. He casts himself adrift on an ocean of ethical uncertainty. Such a person brings anguish into his own life and very often into the lives of his innocent children and others. The Bible says that if a person lifts up his eyes to idols, he shall surely die (Ezekiel 18:12-13).

Pagan decadence has contributed to the ongoing hunger and death by starvation problem. God has always sent His messengers to warn people. God has never left people ignorant about Himself (Romans 1:18-32). But He has declared that tribulation and anguish will fall upon everyone who rejects Him (Romans 2:9). We have only to look back into history, and at what is happening worldwide today to see that what God has decreed does happen. Make no mistake, these are end-times. Jesus said, "For nation will rise against nation, and kingdom against kingdom. And there will be famines, pestilences, and earthquakes in various places" (Matthew 24:7).

---

1. For more on the subject of homelessness and hunger in America, write and ask for my book Beyond Anger and Pity.

2. US Department of Agriculture, *World Agriculture Supply and Demands Estimates* (WASDE) 193, (May 9, 1986).

3. Sudan Relief and Rehabilitation Commission, *Monthly Report* (RICSU, Khartoum, November 1985), as quoted in the book *The Hunger Machine*, p. 52.

10 An Examination of the Assumptions and Myths Surrounding World Hunger

One billion of the world's population is chronically under-nourished and experiences hunger's anguish daily.

There are many commonly held assumptions about hunger and its causes that need examining. Some of them are outright myths and need debunking; others it would be a mistake to dismiss lightly, there are pros and cons to be considered. Hopefully, putting forth this effort to better understand the problems of world hunger will help each of us put hunger's causes in a right perspective.

The Worldwatch Institute, which is an environmental research group who have surveyed the Earth's condition annually since 1984, has issued what is being regarded as perhaps its "grimmest report," "The State of the World 1989."

They make the statement, "We are losing at this point, clearly losing the battle to save the planet," according to the report's chief author, Lester R. Brown. The impending results of what's happening "will shake the world to its foundation," according to Brown.

When you see a headline in the paper that shouts, *"Food situation nearing crisis" Millions could starve: [according to] Institute* [1] what are you supposed to think? Well, be careful what you swallow whole hog, as the old saying goes.

Worldwatch pointed to the heat waves, drought and beach pollution experienced by Americans in the summer of 1988 and said there is a growing awareness of the hazards at hand. That's a true enough statement.

It is being stated by a number of journals, writers and research institutes that the atmosphere is getting hotter, that arable land is disappearing and overpopulation is continuing so that "By the end of the next decade, the die will pretty well be cast." [2]

In particular, researchers point to two critical concerns: Environmental degradation—from the loss of topsoil to a growing scarcity of water, to apparent global warming caused by air pollution—that has cut farm output; and continuing overpopulation. [3]

In this chapter we are going to look at these concerns.

Number One: Overpopulation

Why do people in India and all the Third World countries have so many babies? Don't they know anything at all about birth control? And if we are going to help them, why don't we provide them with birth control information, condoms and devices?

117

Questions like this and statements made about over-population are quite often said in a very condescending manner. Underlying the questions and statements is a good deal of insensitivity, prejudice and misinformation.

If you lived in one of these developing countries and you knew that one out of every five children dies before the age of five, and if your children were looked upon as security in your old age, wouldn't you want to make certain you had survivors? Economic security, which we take for granted, prompts developing world couples to have children. Even in their poverty such parents do think of the future. Children are needed as workers. Poor people, by having lots of children, are making what to them is a rational calculus for survival—the survival of the fittest. Without resources to secure their future, people have to rely on their families.

Moreover, these parents love their children. Don't you think they grieve when they lose these little ones to the effects of malnutrition? Have you ever tried to put yourself in the place of an African mother, for instance, with that pitiful little baby at her breast, and she herself is so emaciated she can hardly stand on her feet? Such mothers hope some of their children will make it. They are proud of their race and their traditions. Can you blame them for wanting progenitors?

In some respects, what the Western World is saying sounds like developing world country people should become fewer so we can become more, as well as richer.

Sometimes people will point to overpopulation as a cause also of pollution in today's world. The truth is that children in our culture, meaning the more "civilized" Western World, pollute the earth probably fifty times more than the average Indian child, for instance, ever will. Most children in our part of the world consume enough food in their lifetime to keep whole Asian villages alive for months.

Cultural considerations also account for large families in certain countries. In Kenya, for instance, men cannot "hold their head high" until they have many sons. That's also true in India. We must be more sensitive to matters of this nature and less quick to judge.

Certain governments, such as in China, seek to limit the families to one child. The traditional preference is to male offspring, so there is evidence of infanticide (i.e., a couple may do away with a little girl baby so they can have another child, hopefully a boy). Undoubtedly this would happen in other countries, as well, if sanctions against having more than one child were to be imposed.

Frances Moore Lappe and Joseph Collins have isolated the twelve most widely circulated myths regarding world hunger and have written definitively about them.[4] In their book, *World Hunger: Twelve Myths,* these authors discuss overpopulation under the chapter title, "Too Many Mouths to Feed." The myth, they explain, like this: *MYTH: Hunger is caused by too many people pressing against finite resources. We must slow population growth before we can hope to alleviate hunger.*

They agree that the question of population is so vital that no one can afford to be the least bit fuzzy in their thinking. So they pose the question: Are population density and and population growth the cause of hunger? And, what is the link between slowing population growth and ending hunger?

They show quite conclusively that if too many people caused hunger, then reducing population density could indeed alleviate it, and that for one factor to cause another, the two must consistently occur together. And population density and hunger do not. They point to China which has only half the cropland per person as India, yet Indians suffer widespread and severe hunger while the Chinese do not. The same comparison could be made between Taiwan and South Korea which each have only half the farmland per person as is found in Bangladesh. No one is pointing to overcrowding as causing hunger in Taiwan and South Korea.

As one surveys the globe, you are hard put to find an absolute correlation between population density and hunger. You could point to the Netherlands, for instance, where there is very little land; yet the people are not going hungry.

Still, most of the world's hungry live in Asia, Africa and Latin America, where populations grow the fastest. What, if any, is the association between the two? After close examination of all the factors, Frances Lappe and Joseph Collins point to hunger and the rapid population growth as both being consequences of similar social realities. In a previous chapter I discussed for you the problem of pervasive poverty as being the most common cause of hunger.

High birthrates reflect people's defensive reaction against enforced poverty. Rapid population growth and corresponding hunger result where societies deny security and opportunity to the majority of their citizens—where adequate land, jobs, education, health care, and old-age security are beyond the reach of most people.[5]

When you are living at the margin of survival, having children who can go out and work or scrounge for food is considered an advantage, not a disadvantage. There is one study done on Bangladesh people, which shows that even by the age of six a boy provides labor and/or income for the family. And by the age of twelve, at the latest, such a son contributes more than he consumes.

Another factor—which is a cultural thing—relates to the fact that bigger families carry more weight in communtiy affairs. So before you spout off another time about over-population as being the cause of world hunger, think twice. There are many aspects to consider. Let's not be simplistic and make hasty blanket generalizations.

It must also be recognized that in many, if not most, of these developing countries where family planning is still relatively new or unknown, women have very little say about what does or does not happen. Where changes have been most rapid and economic well-being of the family has occurred, it has been proven that the women have been successful in regaining control of their lives and their bodies. The changing status of women, from child-bearer to breadwinner, has really revolutionized the lifestyle for families. Some women don't have much opportunity to choose to have fewer children when their husbands have all the power in the family. Some husbands become angry and abuse their wives if they refuse to submit to their sexual demands. In some Third World nations women do not have access to health services that would help educate them. Most of these developing countries are still highly patriarchal societies. Let us be very careful in our assessment of these things.

I repeat what I tried to show in an earlier chapter—only as we unflinchingly face the evidence which tells us that the fate of the world and its hunger problem hinges on the fate of today's poor majorities, only then, as their well-being increases can population growth slow.

Yes, by the year 2000 there will very likely be 10 billion people on earth. Population growth rate is a worrying factor in the developing world. But let it be understood that high birthrates are primarily related to economic uncertainty, not to availability of land. In every country where malnutrition has been reduced and child death rates have decreased, birthrates have also dropped dramatically.[6]

The Bible says for good reason: "Blessed is he that considereth the poor: the LORD will deliver him in time of trouble" (Psalm 41:1).[7]

Number Two: There's Not Enough Food to Go Around

It's hard to believe, but there are a lot of people who honestly believe there isn't enough food in the world to go around. That really can be classified as a myth that needs debunking.

There is plenty of food in the world. There are huge surpluses of unused food in various parts of the world. Actually, the food currently produced each year is more than enough to feed the projected 10 billion people anticipated by the year 2000. Harvests have been increasing at a rate of 2.6 percent annually which is well ahead of the 2 percent population growth rate.[8]

Put another way, the world today produces enough grain alone to provide every human being on the planet with

3,600 calories a day![9] That could make you fat real quick. That estimate doesn't even take into consideration the many other commonly eaten foods—vegetables, beans, nuts, root crops, fruits, grass-fed meats and fish.

Still, hunger in many places throughout the world is real; but scarcity is not. A paradox. Hunger is such an outrage precisely because it is so needless. There are reasons, real causes, but it's not because there isn't enough food to go around.

Television coverage has done a good job of awakening the world to hunger in the Horn of Africa and the Sahel, but some of Africa's worst hunger isn't covered. In Middle Africa, some 50,000 black children starve to death every year; 136 die every day. Yet Zimbabwe and South Africa are exporters of agricultural products, even exporting corn, the basic staple of black families.

Or we could look at India which ranks near the top among Third World agricultural exporters. It is felt that as many as 300 million Indians go hungry, yet the country exports everything from wheat to beef and government officials talk about mounting "surpluses" of wheat and rice—24 million tons in 1985, more than double the entire world's annual food aid shipments in a typical year.[10]

Most of the hungriest countries of the world have enough food for all their people right now. Still, hunger ravages and decimates much of the population. The poor are unable to get their hands on it, or even if they could reach it, to purchase it. It isn't that the food crisis isn't real; it is, and the 1988 drought in the U.S. did cut harvests in some areas up to 30 percent. The real problem lies primarily in man-made and therefore reversible causes. Is pessimism justified? Just how close are we to the earth's limits?

It is quite generally accepted that by the year 2000, the persistence of hunger could be eradicated from every nation on earth. But no one need die from hunger today. In study after study, prestigious international commissions have come to one conclusion: Humanity now possesses the resources, technology and know-how to end hunger.[11]

The Brandt Commission, composed of leaders from seventeen rich and poor countries, conducted a two-year study. A major conclusion reflected wide consensus with this expert community, namely: "Mankind has never before had such ample technical and financial resources for coping with hunger and poverty. The immense task can be tackled once the necessary collective will is mobilized. What is necessary can be done, and must be done."[12]

Human mismanagement of earth's resources, neglect of the needy, the rural farmers and peasants, is a contributing culprit; not shortages and/or insufficient land.

Number Three: Nature Is To Blame

Undeniably, we live in a kind of "media age," paying attention to what hits the evening news and makes the headlines in the paper at the moment. So it is that droughts and famines have caught our attention, just as armed conflicts, violence and civil strife have made us more aware of what's happening around the world.

Therefore, nature gets blamed for starvation. Droughts, floods, earthquakes—these are beyond the control of humankind. Statistics don't lie. So when you read and hear about the millions pushed into destitution by the forces of nature, the assumption is easy to make—the weather causes people to suffer and/or die of hunger.

But if weather is the cause, why don't people in the United States die of starvation when drought hits the Mid-West plains, or a cyclone sweeps through a region? Would an earthquake cause such widespread hunger as to be listed as the cause of death were it to strike in some part of this country?

The truth is that behind each natural disaster lies a multitude of human errors that cause the poorest of the poor to suffer the full impact of nature for they are already living on the edge of subsistence. In the United States, for instance, when a natural disaster occurs, rescue and relief efforts are immediately put into effect. That this does not happen in many parts of the world is a reality that cannot be denied. But to say that nature is the cause, is to fail to recognize how ill-equipped some parts of the world are to handle natural disasters when they do occur on a widespread scale.

Researchers, who went to Ethiopia's highland villages following the 1985 drought to seek out causes of the widespread human suffering they had seen on television, learned some surprising things. They discovered that feudalistic landlordism, hoarding, and governmental policies and indifference contributed greatly to the suffering and the tragic deaths of so many people. It was their conclusion that famines are not necessarily natural disasters, but social disasters, the results of human arrangements, not acts of God.[13]

In the next chapter I will direct your attention to other

assumptions and/or myths regarding the problem of world hunger.

The way people think about hunger can be the greatest obstacle to overcoming it. Something that takes the lives of 35,000 daily needs resolving. That which snuffs out the lives of an estimated 18 children under the age of five per minute needs action.

Our Example

How easily we overlook what the Bible has to say about the poor and hungry. Jesus said to one of the leaders of the Pharisees who invited Him to dinner: "When you give a luncheon or dinner, do not invite your friends, your brothers or relatives, or your rich neighbors; if you do, they may invite you back and so you will be repaid. But when you give a banquet, invite the poor, the crippled, the lame, the blind, and you will be blessed. Although they cannot repay you, you will be repaid at the resurrection of the righteous" (Luke 14:12-14 NIV).

Previous verses relate a parable Jesus told of how invited guests to a wedding feast had, as it were, jostled for the best seats, the place of distinction. The guests were well-to-do, prosperous, smug, a self-satisfied crowd struggling for these chief seats. He showed how despicable this was, and then, turning to his host related that a truly honorable man does not act like that.

Jesus' ideas and words were revolutionary. On this occasion, He was showing the relationship between bad manners and motives and good motives and good manners. The great returns of life will not come in the here and now, they lie in the life that lies beyond.

There was a guest at that banquet who understood what Jesus was saying. I believe his response was very sincere: "Blessed is the man who will eat at the feast in the kingdom of God," he exclaims (vs 15).

Jesus' response tells us how to act upon the message of His parable. The Kingdom of God is a kingdom of grace. God provides the table, the food, no one is excluded. We exclude ourselves when we offer excuses.

Jesus has told us how to treat the poor and needy. When we fail to act upon the example He has given, we, in effect, are offering excuses. Back of our feeble excuses is a lack of desire to obey our Lord. We reveal the poverty in our hearts; we show all to clearly by what we are possessed.

1. As released by the Associated Press and cited in *The South Bend Tribune,* March 21, 1989.
2. Ibid.
3. Ibid.
4. They are co-authors of *World Hunger: Twelve Myths.* Frances Moore Lappe is the author of the international bestseller, *Diet for a Small Planet.*
5. Ibid., p. 25
6. *The Hunger Machine,* p. 22.
7. That entire Psalm speaks of the blessedness that comes to those who consider the plight of the helpless, the weak and the poor. That Psalm and the many other references as to how we are to regard the poor are worthy of our study. God has promised to bless and take care of those who have regard for the poor.
8. Ibid., p. 18
9. *World Hunger. . .,* p. 9.
10. Ibid., p.11.
11. The Hunger Project, *Ending Hunger: An Idea Whose Time Has Come* (New York: Praeger Publishers, 1985), p.16.
12. Ibid., p. 16.
13. *World Hunger . . .,* p. 22.

11 Why Does Hunger Persist?

The earthquake in China in 1976 killed 242,000 people.
Hunger kills that many people every seven days.

By now I hope you have seen that hunger does not exist in isolation. Why does hunger persist? Hunger is held in place by many global forces—economic, social, ideological, political, philosophical, cultural and even psychological.

Food availability is at the very heart of ending hunger. The three aspects of this issue revolve around food production, food shortage and security, and distribution.

We have already looked at food production to some extent, concluding that enough food is currently being produced to feed everyone on planet Earth well. World food production has been increasing steadily for decades. An interesting statistic that came out in 1982 shows the ample availability of grain. That year, the total recorded food production in the world was 3,764 million metric tons. Of that food, about half by weight was grain. This means 1,675 million metric tons—an almost unimaginable amount of food. The grain alone would be enough to fill a 1 foot diameter tube that encircled the earth 742 times. And this amount of grain was produced on this planet **in just one year.**[1]

Enough grain was produced in that year, 1982, to provide each man, woman and child with about two loaves of bread each day.

From 1950 to 1980, annual world production actually doubled. The problem is that these increases in food production have not occurred evenly throughout the world. For instance, in those thirty years, per capita production increased 47 percent in developed countries, but only 15 percent in developing countries. And in sub-Sahara Africa, per capita food production actually declined the last two decades.[2]

The question is sometimes asked: How much land is available for growing food worldwide? There are 13 billion hectares of land in the world, and the total amount of potentially cultivable land is generally agreed to be about 3.2 billion hectares, with only about 1.4 billion now being cultivated. A hectare is 2.47 acres.

The potential for creating new tillable land increases as knowledge, machinery, and power sources are further developed and improved and then put to use and made available to developing countries. There are places in the world today that were once deserts. Technology has brought incredible advances.

You may be wondering about the United States. Are all those dire predictions about the urban population overtaking agriculture land true? Is prime farmland irreversibly lost to agriculture every year through urban sprawl? Are we going to run out of land to grow crops in this country? I found these statistics to be fascinating: Urban areas of the United States occupy only 1 percent of the entire land surface of the country; freeways, highways, turnpikes, cloverleafs, backroads, and service roads, in addition to airports big and small, and 200,000 miles of railroad tracks take up, all told, another 1 percent or a fraction more. Our forests and reforestation, along with pastureland, cover considerably more than half of America's land area.[3]

Moreover, technology has moved us to the place where ruined land can be reclaimed, and water tables can even be raised or lowered. There are many conflicting points of view in regard to these issues. I am trying to point out both sides of the picture. There are certain states and places in the United States that appear to be more in jeopardy than others—for instance, Florida, which produces half of the world's grapefruit and a fourth of the world's oranges, will lose all of its unique and prime lands in less than twenty years if its current conversion rate continues.

Some of us can remember when southern California's beautiful citrus groves were a marvel to behold. Today most of those groves no longer exist. Other such losses have been taking place in other states. But is our planet's resourcefulness waning fast?

There are many more things that could be said about this, suffice to say that economists, historians and those in-the-know agree that there is more than enough energy-producing land, and that the amount of potentially arable land is actually increasing.

Food and the Environment

A myth does exist, however, that says we cannot both feed the hungry and protect our environment. What about pesticides, the clearing of rain forests (deforestation), and soil destruction?

Agriculture technology introduced the "Green Revolution" (mentioned in regard to Mexico and India in particular in an earlier chapter), and has brought tremendous advantages in the production of food over vast areas of the world. That it has caused some ecological problems cannot be denied.

Norman Borlaug, "father" of this "Green Revolution," believes that technology can conserve, even enhance environmental resources. He says, "To produce food for ourselves and other nations, we required 290 million acres of farmland in 1984. To get the same yield while relying on the technology we used thirty years ago, we would have required nearly 600 million acres, or twice the amount used in 1984. This would have resulted in a huge loss of forest and grasslands which not only would have further crowded some animal species into extinction but would have caused other problems as well."[4]

Over 5 billion pounds of pesticides are used annually throughout the world. The human health toll, as a result, is said to be staggering by those who oppose many of these technological advances. Some reports suggest pesticide poisoning may be as high as 1.5 million each year. Pesticides seep into groundwater causing contamination. The threat to health is real, it is claimed, and many accounts are told to substantiate these claims.

Pesticides are expensive and are used primarily by politically influential owners of large commercial farms. Third World governments spend hundreds of millions of dollars annually subsidizing pesticide use.

All the facts point quite conclusively to pesticides as being an environmental health danger. On the other hand, plenty of stories exist showing how modern technology and pesticides have offered advantages to undeveloped countries improving the lot of the farmers. Primitive means of plowing and planting, for instance, limited what a peasant landowner could do. Within rural areas, the poverty problem for many has resolved primarily around low productivity. Control of pest infestations has greatly helped in increasing productivity. In perspective, it must be recognized that even while the agricultural chemical industry has been the whipping boy of environmentalists, the facts also show that gains have been made. An agricultural transformation is taking place in many parts of the world. We must pray that those who till the land and produce the crops will not abuse earth's resources, and that they will use the latest scientific knowledge wisely in order to produce food economically and without harming the environment or the health of mankind.

We must also pray that those who need the help the most, the poor and disadvantaged, will be given access to what is needed to help them. The social reality is that those who are hungry have control over little or no food-producing resources. The powerless are dependent on others. Social changes in these developing countries are desperately needed. Actually, this is where the help of private donor organizations has been the most beneficial.

Food Storage and Security and Distribution

The industrialization of farming in developing countries has consequences both good and bad. Food security for all is what is desperately needed.

While there are those who insist that the "Green Revolution" and advanced technology will put an end to hunger, results in some places disprove these claims. But the economic ground rules governing distribution no doubt have more to do with answering the why than the actual greater production that is afforded. It's interesting that in 1949, President Truman pointed out that "greater production is the key to prosperity and peace. And the key to greater production is a wider and more vigorous application of modern scientific technical knowledge."[5]

But today, while food production advances, hunger widens. Why? The answer is many-dimensional. It has a lot to do with food storage and security and actual distribution.

There are those who are saying that we may now be moving into a very difficult situation where food security may replace military security as the principal preoccupation of many governments in the world. While speculative, this raises some highly interesting points that will bear watching in the years ahead.

Since Bible times, people have found ways to store food

as protection against drought, famine and poor crops. Certainly no one would deny that what is needed today is more visionary end-time Josephs for the end-time problem of world hunger.

Worldwide we need agricultural programs—including storage, security and distribution—that we can all live with. A cornerstone of the food-secure world of Joseph's day was the fortified granaries he had built as a depository for grain, ready to be drawn upon when famine came.

> "Now therefore, let Pharoah select a discerning and wise man, and set him over the land of Egypt.
>
> "Let Pharoah do this, and let him appoint officers over the land, to collect one-fifth of the produce of the land of Egypt in the seven plentiful years.
>
> "And let them gather all the food of those good years that are coming, and store up grain under the authority of Pharaoh, and let them keep food in the cities.
>
> "Then that food shall be as a reserve for the land for the seven years of famine which shall be in the land of Egypt, that the land may not perish during the famine."
>
> So the advice was good in the eyes of Pharoah and in the eyes of all his servants.
>
> And the Pharoah said to his servants, "Can we find such a one as this, a man in whom is the Spirit of God?"
>
> Then Pharoah said to Joseph, "Inasmuch as God has shown you all this, there is no one as discerning and wise as you.
>
> "You shall be over my house, and all my people shall be ruled according to your word; only in regard to the throne will I be greater than you."
>
> And Pharaoh said to Joseph, "See, I have set you over all the land of Egypt."
>
> —Genesis 41:33-41 (NKJ)

The Bible shows that Joseph was able to nourish his father and his brothers, and all their household, with bread. He provided for them (Genesis 47:12).

Famine watchers and researchers are in agreement—the key component of any program of world food storage is an effective system of food storage which can serve as a buffer against lean times.[6] According to the Food and Agriculture Organization (FAO), the amount of grain storage necessary to guarantee world food security is 17 to 18 percent of total annual world consumption.[7]

Questions arise as to who should hold these reserves and who should distribute them when the needs arise. An internationally coordinated system of food security would appear to be the answer. The logistics and problems this presents are formidable.

Such are some of the problems, issues and myths surrounding the world food hunger problem. There are those who say that justice and production are competing goals. Myth or reality? Others say the free market can end hunger, that if governments just got out of the way, the problems wouldn't exist as they do today.

Still others insist that more foreign aid will help the hungry. Actually, foreign aid is only going to be as good as the recipient government. The scandals of the Marcos regime in the Philippines is a classic example of a foreign policy that actually ended up bankrolling a ruthless, greedy ruler.

As Frances Moore Lappe and Joseph Collins point out, "Where the recipient government answers only to a narrow economic elite, our aid not only fails to reach the hungry, it girds the very forces working against them."[8]

The beneficial results of food-aid programs have been proven, but there exist many accounts of abuses, of the food being blackmarketed at exorbitant prices lining the coffers of heartless and unscrupulous men, and even of food rotting on docks.

That is why the work of private donor organizations is so important; that is why I believe God has called into existence our own work, The End-Time Joseph Program to Feed the Hungry.

---

1. *Ending Hunger*, p. 96

2. As cited in the book *Ending Hunger*, p. 96.

3. Ibid., p. 104.

4. Ibid., p. 141.

5. Ibid., p. 125.

6. Ibid., p. 156.

7. Ibid., p. 157.

8. *World Hunger: Twelve Myths*. . ., p.113.

12 Routing the Enemy Hunger

"In my judgment the Christian faith does not lend itself to much preaching or talking. It is best propagated by living it and applying it. . . When will you Christians really crown Jesus Christ as the Prince of Peace and proclaim him through your deeds as the champion of the poor and the oppressed?"
                                                              Ghandi

How would you feel if an earthquake were to strike San Francisco and kill 35,000 people in one day?

If a virus descended on Chicago, killing 18 children a minute, week after week after week, would you feel concern?

If nuclear weapons exploded in the capitals of the world's major industrial countries, killing 13 million people and maiming and injuring a billion more in the surrounding areas, what would you think? Would you want to respond somehow?

These are terrible tolls and we pray these events never occur. Yet, the persistence of world hunger as an ongoing condition is real and it is taking that kind of toll—1 billion chronically undernourished; 13-18 million dead a year; 35,000 dying daily from hunger and its effects; 24 dying per minute, 18 of them children.

Hunger has stepped into the thinking of millions around the world as they have encountered the specter in its various forms. This includes those responsible for administering foreign aid programs, and it includes private donor organizations. These are people who are seeking ways to end the problem of hunger. Many who are working most effectively can be found in the private donor organizations. Our own End-Time Joseph Program to Feed the Hungry will for sure be a leader in reaching the multitudes of hungry people.

When going into an emergency situation, the greatest immediate need is for food, of course, and that is what is supplied. However, we sponsor other programs with great effectiveness. These include medical assistance, provisions of blankets and clothing and other needs.

In these ways hunger has been routed, peoples' lives saved, and the needs of people in many places have been met.

Many of us, as Christian donor organizations, work together in emergency-aid partnering. If one organization has access to supplies and equipment for a particular needy spot, others provide the financial help. As others have pointed out, it is amazing how much can be accomplished when you are not consumed with who gets the credit.

Donor organizations such as ours work collaboratively

with corporations and private donors assuring the philanthropic community of trustworthy means of making certain their actual donations of money and/or product gets into the hands of the truly needy. As a worldwide ministry, LeSEA has, for over twenty years, helped people in many countries, including monetary and physical help. We have ongoing direct aid programs into Poland, the Philippines, Sri Lanka, Africa, Haiti, South and Central America, and other countries and U.S. cities as the needs come to our attention.

A Pastor-to-Pastor Program

When the Lord gave me the vision in Jerusalem in the fall of 1987, speaking to my heart and telling me we were to specifically begin an End-Time Joseph Program to Feed the Hungry, God said this was to be a pastor-to-pastor program. We were to call for 10,000 pastors to challenge world hunger. The Lord showed me that these pastors were to lead their churches in responding to the biblical mandate to feed the hungry and "set at liberty those who are oppressed" (Luke 4:18).

The plan has proven to be very successful. Pastors around the world have responded. We have pastor/directors in Canada, Europe, Australia, New Zealand, Africa, the Orient, Central America and, of course, throughout the United States. Many of our pastors have accompanied us on feeding trips, going into refugee camps and places where pastors are ministering locally in the hunger pockets of the world.

Prior to entrance into a given locale, we secure a

guarantee from the government of the country in which we want to distribute food. This guarantee insures that we can hand the food directly to local pastors and they will be able to give it to the people.

For instance, in Zimbabwe, at a feeding area, we met with the regional administrator and his four assistants. The first thing he asked me was, "Why can't you give me the food and let us distribute it seeing that I am the government administrator for this area?"

I answered him kindly, but candidly, telling him that this was not food given by public solicitation, but that this was food donated by pastors and their churches, and that we were not permitted to give it to anyone but a pastor and his church. He thought for a moment and said, "Well, I will observe."

And so, in his own jeep, he took us to the area. There were many hundreds of people present, and he sat very patiently while I preached to the people.

Then we went to a school building where the food was stored, and pastors and elders of churches began to call out the names of people and the distribution began.

We took the local administrators into one of the rooms of the humble school building and served them some of the lunch we had brought with us, which they greatly enjoyed. He and the other administrators watched the happy people receiving their bags of maize with shouting, rejoicing and singing. It was so thrilling.

As the government administrator took us back to our private airplane, he said, "You can do this anytime. This is the most beautiful thing I have ever seen, and you have done it so beautifully, without any kind of prejudice. You have made our people happy, and besides that, you have prayed for and healed our sick."

In this particular distribution, we dispensed 60.5 U.S. tons of maize meal and left an additional 44 tons which has been distributed in Malawi by the Tippetts in Blantyre.

In addition, we left 1,200 blankets which were distributed in Malawi. Blankets are used to cover their nakedness and for protection from the nighttime cold. It can get very cold there at night.

You cannot begin to imagine the deprivation of these people. The things we take so much for granted—blankets, roofs, walls and windows in our homes, changes of clothing, shoes, running water, toilets and toilet paper—just to mention some basic necessities. These things are, for the most part, unknown to these people.

In one of the camps I saw a large hole in the ground and was informed this was their source of water. I brought up a containerful. It was murky. Not the kind of water you and I would even think of drinking. Yet this was all they had. In many parts of Africa they have not had rainfall for a long, long time.

A Three-Pronged Approach

Ours is a three-pronged approach to rout both spiritual and physical hunger. Not only does the Body of Christ in these faraway corners of the globe need food to sustain them, but they need spiritual help and encouragement as well. We try to do that.

God spoke to my spirit and said that He would raise up many spiritual men and women who would respond to their pastors and support this Feed-the-Hungry program; that pastors and churches were searching for a place to put funds to strengthen the universal Body of Christ and win the lost to salvation.

So our program has three distinct outreaches:

1. We feed the hungry.

2. We strengthen churches with pastors' seminars.

3. We strengthen the people through evangelistic crusades with proclamation of the gospel, spiritual transformation—setting people free from bondage to the devil and demonic power—and prayer for the sick and oppressed.

The Lord said we must never use just a one-pronged approach, such as only delivering food, but we must use the three-pronged approach, and this will insure vital strength and victory.

I am always so moved when the pastors on the field where we have been ministering introduce me. Usually they say something like this: "This is the man whose heart of compassion has led him to come to help us. He comes from the United States. He is a long way from his home."

When I thank pastors like this, I say to the people, "I am here representing many hundreds of Christians from around the world. This food did not come from rich people, it came from people who want to love you just like Jesus told us to love one another. We have deep compassion for those who suffer. We come in Jesus' name—He came from heaven to bless us and we are here to bless you. Someday we can all live together with Jesus in heaven. There won't be any difference in the color of our faces, and there won't be anymore hunger and sickness. . ."

God has blessed our approach, and we find favor with government and church leaders wherever we go. We met with provincial leaders in Quelamane (Mozambique) at a cabinet meeting. They told us that in the recent civil war 1,000 schools, 200 hospitals, and 50 bridges had been destroyed in the country. We learned that there were 600,000 displaced persons in Mozambique in a hundred refugee camps.

These stories could be repeated in many places throughout the world. Hunger is dehumanizing and debilitating, and it is experienced by one out of every five people on the planet. If hunger were eliminated in India alone, as much as one-third of the world's hunger would be ended.

Needed: Committed Action

The world's communtiy of experts, however, agree that by the year 2,000, the persistence of hunger could be eradicated from every nation on earth. Ours is an incredibly fertile and productive planet right now, and we could produce much more. This earth is already producing more than enough food to feed hundreds of millions more than are now alive. No one need die of hunger.

What is needed is committed action on the part of the world communtiy. I find it of tremendous importance that the world's Christian community has responded and are responding as they are.

Breakthroughs can be achieved that will alleviate much of the hunger. The question that is being asked is: "Which pathway will nations and the world community pursue to ensure that enough food in the right places is available to all?"

The End-Time Joseph Program to Feed the Hungry is committed to a compassionate response. The Bible is clear in setting forth the responsibility of those who have toward those who have not. We are told in 1 John 3:17-18 that "If anyone has this world's goods—resources for sustaining life—and sees his brother and fellow believer in need, yet closes his heart of compassion against him, how can the love of God live and remain in him?

"Little children, let us not love [merely] in theory or in speech, but in deed and in truth—in practice and in sincerity" (AMP).

We can't do everything, but we can do something. And with God's help, and the help of His people, we will continue to seek ways to help rout hunger from planet Earth, and to ease the suffering of the hungry and the needy. Christians know the truth of these words: "It is more blessed to give than to receive" (Acts 20:35).

13 The Challenge

God is not stuck on a world view that has geographical, political and racial boundaries.

This world in which we live presents many challenges. You can call them problems if you wish. Many do. But an old Chinese proverb suggests a way of looking at problems that appeals to me. It says to regard "problems" as "golden opportunities."

These challenges range far afield—from outer space to small bugs crawling on the face of the earth. Both are important. Each has their place. But in a world that spends hundreds of millions on their military establishments, while millions are hungry and actually die of hunger-related causes at the same time, the greatest challenge is the welfare of people. The question remains: Has it been, and is it?

Military Spending, the Arms Race and Hunger

Developing nations, as well as developed nations, spend substantial sums on their military forces, nuclear weapons and appropriate delivery systems (long-range bombers, ground-and-submarine-launched ballistic missiles, and air-launched cruise missiles). Does it come as a surprise when I tell you that some of the poorest countries of the world actually allocate between 2 and 10 percent of their GNP (gross national product) for military purposes?

National security is a priority. Internal stability and territorial integrity must be maintained through strong military forces in these developing countries. Hunger problems often increase amidst the chaos and social upheaval and accompany revolutions. Funds that could help put an end to poverty and hunger are pre-empted by military uses. This is a reality.

We've all heard figures on what is spent in this country for arms. One such figure says $800 million is spent every day on weapons we will never use! That is so enormous as to defy one's imagination. I have heard it stated another way: In one day America's military spending equals a full year's expenditures of the UN's food and health programs.

The arms race not only presents terrible danger to mankind, but it draws resources away from that which could be used to enhance the quality of life for millions of people. When a government spends more on militarisation of society than it does on education or health, it plays havoc with production of food and other necessities of life.

The challenge is to safeguard the welfare of nations without depriving the majority of the people of their basic human needs and rights. Can it be accomplished? What a golden opportunity!

Those who believe military spending is in the best interests of society say that social benefits will follow. They point to communist regimes who perpetuate conditions in which human suffering, including hunger, flourishes. They say weaker nations must be shielded from Soviet aggression.

Journalist Norman Podhoretz explains it like this: "Human rights have invariably fared worse under Communism than under the regimes it has replaced. Are the Cubans today better off than they were under Batista? Ask the many thousands who have already left and the countless others who are clamoring to get out. Are the South Vietnamese better off under the rule of the North than they were under Thieu? Ask the boat people. Are the Cambodians better off as Kampucheans? Ask the grave. These are the most hideous illustrations of the rules, but it is important to understand that the horrors perpetrated by the Communists in power are not accidental or arbitrary. They follow from the totalitarian nature of Communist regimes."[1]

Development in developing countries can best take place under conditions of order and stability. Crises situations are not conducive to social justice. Revolutions are caused by revolutionaries—people with guns and weapons. Violence and terrorism have brought unimaginable suffering to vast numbers of the victimized.

Both proponents and opponents of military spending have as their goal the creation of a secure and stable world. The challenge is how best to achieve this. The root causes of the world's underlying tensions must be removed and/or resolved. Can this be accomplished? Another golden opportunity!

The World Solution:
A New International Economic Order

There is a school of thought which holds that to promote development and to end hunger and poverty, a New International Economic Order (NIEO) must be established in place of the current international economic order.

The existing and widening disparities between the richest and the poorest nations promotes denial of equality of opportunity. The gap between the rich and poor in the communist world is appalling. (See Appendix D in the back of this book.)

The challenge is to narrow the gap. Great changes—"A veritable revolution"—are needed to correct the problems of the current order, according to economists and world watchers. Proponents of the NIEO offer a variety of views and perspectives about the goals of development for developing countries, the responsibility of some nations for others, how best to promote justice and equity, and proposals to reform the complex monetary and financial interactions among nations.

Forums and debates surround these issues. At the very center of these issues is the primary issue of the persistence of hunger.

A Changing World

These are certainly challenges. The world is changing. It has changed dramatically since the day when I, as a seventeen-year-old boy, felt the call of God upon my life and began my global trek. For years, the soles of my shoes slapped the streets in the great cities and tiny villages of the world as I responded to God's call upon my life. I have preached the gospel in over a hundred countries and have ministered in more than a thousand of the world's cities. Yes, I have observed great changes firsthand.

Just thirty years ago, the population of the world stood at less than 3 billion. Today there are a little more than 5 billion. Conservative estimates say the global population may rise to 10 billion over the next century. If the many challenges raised in this book are not seized as golden opportunities, and something isn't done to bring about revolutionary changes, then the outlook for the future and the problem of hunger looms as very bleak.

But I am not a pessimist. Never have been and never will be. We have a God in heaven who is concerned about people here on earth. The challenge that presents itself is that of getting food and resources from places of plenty to places of need.

When Jesus left this earth, He left behind instructions on how we, as stewards of this planet, were to care for it and the people who populated it. Our mandate is plainly spelled out in ever so many places. As I have said before, we can't do everything, but each of us can do something. And together, that something can made a big difference. It can impact the lives of suffering people in ever so many places.

No effort in the name of Jesus is small. Little is much when God is in it. Just to look at Jesus' life is to be challenged to seize the opportunities. His was the perspective of doing what he could for those who came within His scope of awareness. We can do that.

The Challenge That Surrounds Us Today

In Mark 6:35-42, the Lord Jesus in speaking to His disciples said, "Give them something to eat."

They were looking out at a minimum of five thousand men *besides* women and children! The disciples and the people had listened intently to Jesus as He taught and now they were all hungry. That's when Jesus addressed His disciples and told them to give the people something to eat.

What a challenge to the disciples! Now Jesus does not, and did not, play games. He meant that His disciples had the ability to feed those people.

Would they be equal to it? Are we equal to it today? Perhaps the greatest emergency in the history of mankind today is millions dying of hunger. Is the Church going to rise to confront this emergency? God didn't command the governments of the world to feed the hungry, He said His people were to do it (see Matthew 25:31-46).

Jesus discovered that His disciples didn't have the power of will, emotion or mind to feed those people. They complained about environment and conditions.

As I think about some of the existing problems in the world that we have looked at in this book, I am reminded of these disciples. It's not that the problems then weren't real, and it's not that they aren't real today. They are. But what the disciples forgot, and what we so often forget, is that we have a God who is greater than the greatest of problems and seeming obstacles.

The difference between Jesus and His disciples is the word "compassion." Jesus had filled the people's empty hearts with truth, and now He was challenged with the need to fill their empty bodies with food. The Bible shows that this happened because "He [Jesus] was moved with compassion" (vs. 34).

Jesus refused to send those people away with just blessing their hearts. He had taught them the Word. He had healed their sick, and He simply would not send them away to "faint on the way."

Accepting the Challenge

Now what if these disciples had accepted the challenge to feed those five thousand men plus women and children? They would have changed history. The account would have followed them wherever they went in the days ahead. Who knows what might have resulted in terms of the impact of their message in the days following Christ's crucifixion and resurrection and the beginning of the early Church!

However, through unbelief and fear, they backed away and Jesus Himself made history!

But this was an emergency moment for twelve disciples. They had already seen miracles of every kind; they had even seen the dead raised. But because they did not have the material substance in their hands, they refused to believe, and they failed in their encounter with an emergency.

The challenge for us is to hear God speaking to the Church today. He is saying, "Give the world's hungry something to eat."

If Christians around the world rallied to those words of Jesus, think what the impact could be to a watching world! What a golden opportunity!

It's one thing to bring God's love to the lost, but when a man's stomach is in pain because he is so terribly hungry, and when his wife is so weak she can barely sit up, and when their children who are left are nothing but skin and bones, it's awfully hard for people like that to hear the Gospel. The challenge is for God's people to become God's Word for these victims of hunger and poverty.

We do it by giving and going. All of us can give something, some can give more than others; and some of us can go. We can give them food to nourish their bodies, to strengthen them and help them regain their health, and we can leave behind the tangible means whereby they can sustain themselves. And then through our pastor contacts, we can have the assurance that they will be ministered to spiritually as well.

The Apostle Paul has a message for us. It is straightforward and true: "Command those who are rich in this present world not to be arrogant nor to put their hope in wealth, which is so uncertain, but to put their hope in God, who richly provides us with everything for our enjoyment. Command them to do good, to be rich in good deeds, and to be generous and willing to share. In this way, they will lay up treasure for themselves as a firm foundation for the coming age, so that they may take hold of the life that is truly life" (1 Timothy 6:17-19 NIV).

14 Will World Hunger End?

"No servant can serve two masters. Either he will hate the one and love the other, or he will be devoted to the one and despise the other. You cannot serve both God and money. . .but God knows your hearts. What is highly valued among men is detestable in God's sight"
(Luke 16:13, 15b NIV).

Will hunger as a world problem ever end? The question is often asked. There are many world organizations, economists, agriculturists and specialists of all kinds who do nothing but study this issue seeking ways to end the hunger problem. And progress has been and is being made.

There is no scarcity of perspectives, approaches and thinking on the problem of the persistence of hunger. These varying points of view have generated many policies, projects and experiments for eradicating hunger. There is already available, and in place, a wealth of expertise and knowledge that has substantially advanced the cause of the hungry.

Since 1900, seventy-five countries have ended hunger within their borders. Of that number, forty-one have accomplished this since 1960. That's considered real progress. More than half the world's population lives in countries that no longer suffer from the persistence of hunger.[1]

How is the existence of hunger measured? The most widely accepted standard of measurement is called the IMR (infant mortality rate). This is done by measuring the number of infants per thousand who are born live and who die before their first birthday. Hunger is considered a chronic, persistent, society-wide problem when the IMR of a country is greater than fifty—meaning when more than fifty children per thousand die in the first year of their life.

This is a very interesting study to pursue. Perhaps you are wondering which seventy-five countries have succeeded in bringing their IMR below fifty. They are, for the most part, as is to be expected, those countries that are considered "developed," meaning North America, Europe, and parts of Asia and Latin America. Not surprisingly, hunger persists as a basic issue in every African country with a population greater than 1 million. But, in 1900, this was true for every country in the world.

What Has Worked to End Hunger?

What are some of the things that have worked to help bring an end to hunger as a national program in various countries? Basically, it has been a combination of pioneering medical, educational and developmental activities, including a wide range of agricultural techniques.

Basic preventive-health measures (immunization programs, clean-water supplies), and nutrition-improving measures were used. Additional successful measures included: increasing basic education and literacy; redistribution of wealth, land and power; promoting industrial developmment; increasing agricultural production; and improving food distribution, storage and delivery systems.

There is no single prescribed way of achieving the end of hunger in a society. Some countries have focused on land reform (transferring land ownership to the peasants), others have emphasized food subsidies, collectivized agriculture, or privately owned "family farms."

The achievements of such countries as Taiwan, China, Sri Lanka, and the other seventy-five nations where hunger has ended points the way providing examples for the end of hunger elsewhere. And so, in answer to the question, "Is the world progressing toward ending hunger?" there is recognition and a growing consensus that we already have the necessary resources, technology and know-how to end hunger on our planet in this century. But will it happen?

What Is Missing in the Global Effort to End Hunger?

I find it very interesting that even world hunger watchers—those most well informed—say that the end of hunger is now a possibility, but it is not a promise. "It is not something that will happen inevitably, regardless of what we do or don't do. Hunger can end—but that is not the same as saying it will end," write the compilers of the book *Ending Hunger*.[2]

Breakthroughs have been made, and we are grateful for

that. But there is quite general agreement that what is missing in the global effort to end hunger is commitment—a commitment to actually insure that what can be done shall be done. Commitment is considered the missing ingredient.[3]

The secular world is admitting it. I believe it is time the Christian world admits it also. Commitment is an important word in the vocabulary of Christians. Nothing great has ever been achieved in anything without commitment. The question is in order: To what or whom are you committed?

---

1. *Ending Hunger*, p. 384

2. *Enging Hunger*, p. 393

3. Ibid.

15 "There Will Be Famines and Troubles"

"For nation will rise against nation, and kingdom against kingdom. And there will be earthquakes in various places, and there will be famines and troubles. These are the beginnings of sorrows" (Mark 13:8 NKJ).

There was a time when I was one of the younger evangelists in the world, but today I stand in the midst of God's people as one of your elder evangelists. I have seen great changes come throughout the world, and I say to you, as our Lord said, "Watch therefore, watch! Be ready!" (See Matthew 24:42.)

Jesus said the days preceding His second coming would be ushered in by many signs. When you hear of nations rising against nations, and kingdoms rising against kingdoms, do you think of the approaching end of this world? What have we witnessed in recent years in Africa? Has it not been kingdom against kingdom? Kingdoms are territorial units within a country.

Jesus said this would happen, and that there would be famines and troubles. Man's inhumanity to man. SIN. The curse of hunger a result. Satan using food deprivation as a means of tormenting the human race.

Will hunger end? Man may speculate about this, but the Bible supplies the answer. We applaud any and every effort to eradicate hunger, and we are committed to doing all we can to ease the anguish and pain of suffering humanity. We will continue to minister in Jesus' name wherever and whenever we can worldwide.

"The Day of the Lord. . ."

Will it be better or will there be a worldwide crisis? The ancient Hebrew prophet, Joel, foresaw a time when whole nations would be scrapping for a scrap of bread for their people. He speaks of it as "the day of the Lord."

Alas for that day!
    For the day of the Lord is near,
    it will come like destruction from
    the Almighty.
Has not the food been cut off
    before our very eyes—
joy and gladness
    from the house of our God?
The seeds are shriveled beneath the clods.
The storehouses are in ruins,
    the granaries have been broken down,
    for the grain has dried up.
How the cattle moan!
    The herds mill about
    because they have no pasture;

even the flocks of the sheep are suffering.
To you, O Lord, I call,
 for fire has devoured the open pastures
 and flames have burned up all the trees of the field.
Even the wild animals pant for you;
 the streams of water have dried up
 and fire has devoured the open pastures.
—Joel 1:15-20 (NIV)

Succeeding passages tell of the pain of the people whose "faces shall gather blackness" (Joel 2:6). "Blackness" of the face occurs when famine strikes and hunger's effects are ravishing the body.

Elsewhere, as in Jeremiah 4:28, and Lamentations 4:8-10, black is indicative of famine scourging as a blighting plague. In prophesying of the siege and defeat of Jerusalem, the prophet spoke of the appearance of the people as being "blacker that soot,"

> They go unrecognized in the streets; Their skin clings to their bones, it has become as dry as wood. Those slain by the sword are better off than those who die of hunger; for these pine away, stricken for lack of the fruits of the field. The hands of the compassionate women have cooked their own children; they became food for them. . .
> —Lamentations 4:8-10 (NKJ).

Bible teachers are in agreement, the black horse of Revelation 6:5-6, is famine. Famine as described in that passage is one of the six seal judgments of the end days. In fact, it is spoken of as being the third seal. I think we had better pay attention.

We went to Poland in the fall of 1988 to deliver food and minister to the people. I had been in central Poland, in

Lodz, in the mid-1930s when Howard Carter, veteran English missionary, and I traveled from one country to another in crude Russian springless wagons over hole-pocked, bumpy roads and cobblestone streets. Sometimes we nearly froze from the icy rain and bad weather. The poverty of the people was so readily apparent, but God's presence was so very real in the meetings. The hallelujahs which came spontaneously from these radiant Christians caused us to rejoice. Some of the people we were told came to our meetings having walked sixty-five miles in snow, some wearing shoes made from strips of bark from willow trees, and stockings made of rags wrapped around their legs. We slept with the people in their poor farmhouses, and had the lice to prove it. The food was beyond description, but all that is nothing when you can be a blessing to even one of God's children.

Poland was the home then of a few million of Abraham's descendants. These Polish Jews were easily identifiable with their long beards, little black caps, and quaint dress. We could not know then the fate of these beautiful Polish people, that in a few years, the Nazis would reign destruction on the land, torture, kill and take the people captive. While we were there we were told every so often that the people already were laboring under severe strain, that one of the churches had been closed by the government. But it was far different from the Poland that was to emerge after the enormous destruction and suffering that took place during World War II.

In January 1982, Poland was in its second month of martial law, and by a single stroke of a general's pen the price of food was trebled, and in some instances it was quadrupled. *Newsweek* (Jan. 25, 1982) characterized Poland as "a nation awash in black." These Poles were being visited by "the black horse" of famine. When I was there on this last trip, I couldn't help asking, "Will it happen again? Will the Polish people experience more suffering as the result of this black horse at some point in the future?

"Will there be any place on the face of the earth that isn't touched by this black horse and its rider?"

Laudatory as are the efforts to eradicate hunger—and such efforts must always continue, and Christian donor organizations must seek to do all they can—but I repeat, laudatory as are such efforts, the black horse is running throughout the earth. Even people like world-renowned biologist Dr. Paul Erlich of Stanford University, has said, "There is not the slightest hope of escaping a disastrous time of famines," for from this moment onward, "it is shockingly apparent that the battle to feed man will end in a rout."

I don't know Dr. Erlich's religious orientation, but it is almost as though he is speaking from knowledge of end-time prophecies. To be sure, many who speak of ongoing famine and a future major crisis, are speaking from a vantage point that looks at the many issues surrounding world hunger covered in this book. They speak of "irreversible shortages," that "Planet Earth is no longer a sustainable society," of topsoil turning sterile or eroding away, of the ongoing degrading poverty that is endemic in so many places on this earth, of over-fishing and pollution, of "something awesome happening to the weather" world-wide, and things of this nature. These are realities, although for every reality mentioned, there is another side of the coin (and I have tried to show both sides of the picture throughout this book).

What Is the Real Cause for Famine?

Is there yet another aspect to this picture of world famine that is not being addressed by and large? I believe there is.

The Apostle Paul spoke of it. While we don't generally associate the apostle with prophetic utterances, still there it is in 2 Timothy 3. As Paul recites a catalogue of the godless behavior that will characterize the last days, he includes unthankfulness.

He warns that "there will be terrible times in the last days," perilous times, times of great stress and trouble, hard to deal with and hard to bear. Sober words. Words that should make you sit up and take notice.

God is not pleased with ungrateful people. There is plenty of biblical evidence to support my statement from the Old all the way through the New Testament. The Apostle Paul, in another instance, in writing to the Christians at Thessalonica, in speaking of the Lord's return, told them how to behave and what to do, and he emphasized this need to be thankful. "In everything give thanks," he said, "for this is the will of God. . ." (1 Thessalonians 5:18).

Biblical Ethics and Contemporary Society

Have Christians by and large been faithful to biblical revelation? Have the teachings of the Bible been faithfully taught? Are they being practiced?

I have said before that blanket generalizations are unwise. So when I say that I do not believe the standards of social justice set down for us in the scriptures have been applied in our contemporary society, I am running the risk of offending some of God's people.

Some of you reading this have sought to live out your lives in obedience to the revealed will of God. I am not speaking of you. But there has been and is great sinful neglect of the needy and an almost total disregard for what the Bible teaches by multitudes of people who call themselves Christians. Let me be quick to point out that the Bible doesn't necessarily charge the "haves" of this world with direct oppression of the "have nots," but it points out with painful clarity how the needy have been oppressed by the failure of those who have it within their power to make their lives better.

So when I tell you that the God who loves the poor is angry with those who neglect them, your argument is with God, not me. More than 60 percent of Americans are overweight—it totals more than 1.5 billion pounds of blubber that we could well do without. Canadians weigh too much also—more than a hundred million pounds in fact. How did we get that way?

Well, for sure we didn't manage this by sitting on the parched ground, naked, with an empty bowl in our hands. We are too fat, too rich and too uncaring. We know very little about sacrifice, suffering and doing without.

We spend annually more than 15 million dollars on products that are supposed to help us lose weight. And to cover and conceal our rolls of fat in efforts to make ourselves look better, we spend more than 22 billion on cosmetics. We are living sumptuously in comparison to much of the world.

Yet, there are famines in places of the world that we could

fly to overnight. The Bible says there will be famines in diverse places, meaning many places (see Mark 13:8).

The Lord of History Has a Word About This

There is an account in the Old Testament of the destruction of Sodom that we usually associate with one thing—we blame their gross sexual perversions. The prophet Ezekiel was told by God to confront Jerusalem with her detestable practices, prostitution and promiscuity. This he did, and in pointing to all this, the prophet goes on to say that Jerusalem copied the ways of her sister city, Sodom. "Now this was the sin of your sister Sodom: She and her daughters were arrogant, overfed and unconcerned; they did not help the poor and needy. They were haughty and did detestable things before me. Therefore I did away with them. . ." (Ezekiel 16:49-50 NIV).

We remember Sodom's sexual misconduct; we forget her sinful unconcern for the poor. Read the indictment again—Sodom was "arrogant, overfed and unconcerned." I say to you, our thinking as Christians needs an overhaul.

Why does famine persist? Why will it persist on into the future? Because we are basically quite indifferent to the plight of so much of the rest of the world as we bask in our creature comforts.

Christians worldwide have failed in responding to clear biblical mandates on how to treat the hungry, the poor, and the needy.

Let us hear the words spoken by Daniel to the king: "Therefore, O king, let my counsel be acceptable to you; break off your sins by being righteous, and your iniquities by showing mercy to the poor" (Daniel 4:27 NKJ).

In the next chapter, we will look at the biblical texts that lay before us exactly what our responsibility and our attitude should be.

16 Clogged Arteries of Compassion

The God revealed in the Bible can clearly be seen as the Liberator of the needy and oppressed.

The United States loses enough people to heart disease each year to equal six atomic bombs at Hiroshima, or ten Vietnam wars, or ten Vietnam memorial monuments stacked one on top of the other. Present statistics reveal that one fifteen-year-old in 158 will succumb to heart disease.[1]

In spite of some recent decreases in heart disease mortality, it is still the leading American killer claiming about two lives every minute. Nearly 1 million Americans died from cardiovascular disease in 1986, almost as many as cancer, accidents and all other causes of death combined. Still other researchers claim that 1.5 million Americans are struck by heart disease each year.

While the figures vary, the facts remain—heart disease is a modern problem. At the turn of the century, the leading causes of death were pneumonia, influenza and tuberculosis. In 1911, blocked arteries were not a problem.

There are more than 1.25 million heart attacks every year, and over 500,000 deaths occur from them. The costs are astronomical. Illness and death from heart disease in a recent year had an estimated tab of 49 billion in lost productivity and health-care costs. Why does this problem exist as it does today?

Some of the precursors leading to heart attacks are excessively high blood cholesterol levels, with more than 60 million Americans having that as a health problem; high blood pressure (58 million) or at least a quarter of the population; and 34 million people who are significantly overweight.

When Yankee Stadium was remodeled during the '70s, nine thousand seats were lost because the average human posterior had increased by three inches in width. That would actually be funny if it weren't so serious.

So we have a major health problem. South Americans, Africans and Asians do not have heart disease like we do in America. Greeks, Italians and Japanese do not have heart disease until they move to America. But the United States, Canada, the British Isles, and Scandanavia share a common life style, and they all have heart problems. Finland is No. 1 in heart disease in the world; America is No. 3. I submit to you that we have a heart problem in this country and much of the world. Moreover, I submit to you that not only is it clogged arteries leading to heart disease and heart attacks, but much of the world suffers from clogged arteries of compassion.

Both our physical heart problems, and our spiritual condition can be traced to our life styles. Actually, they are problems that can be dealt with. But it requires a commitment to change. And as all this relates to the hungry of the world, it will require a commitment that says, "I care. I will show compassion. I will become familiar with what the Bible says about caring for the afflicted, the poor, the hungry, the needy, and I will respond in obedience."

Lending to the Lord

The writer of Proverbs declared that "He who is kind to the poor lends to the Lord" (Proverbs 19:17 NIV).

It is another way of saying that pity for the poor is to identify with them in their circumstances.

God's kindness to the poor and oppressed is seen at the time of the exodus when He freed the people from their Egyptian taskmasters (Exodus 3:7-8; 6:5-7; 20:2; Deuteronomy 5:6; 26:5-8). He used a man to end this suffering and injustice. That man was Moses. The importance of the human instrumentality is seen. God is concerned that oppressed people know Him as a Deliverer.

Moses-like men and women are needed today to help liberate the poor.

Woe to Those Who Turn Aside From the Needy

God will not tolerate mistreatment of the poor forever. That is the explosive message of the Old Testament prophets. To look at the books of Amos, Hosea, Micah, Isaiah and Jeremiah is to hear God thundering out his anger through these prophets at the injustices foisted upon the poor. It was to become the downfall of the chosen people in the northern kingdom; it was to send them into captivity at the hands of the Assyrians.

I can't help but wonder if, in looking at the scandals that have rocked the Christian world in recent years, God in heaven hasn't called to His side the prophet Amos, and hasn't said to him, "Look at those cows, don't they remind you of the women of Bashan?"

The reference is to Amos 4. "Hear this word, you cows [women] of Bashan on Mount Samaria, you women who oppress the poor and crush the needy and say to your husbands, 'Bring us some drinks!' " (vs. 1 NIV).

The poor were left without hope because of the oppression of the rich (Amos 5:10-15).

There were shocking extremes of wealth and poverty even as there is today. Hosea, who was a contemporary of Amos, spoke of the people eating and never having enough (Hosea 4:10). He refers to their idolatry and economic exploitation of the poor. They were faithless and merciless. "Hear the word of the LORD, you Israelites, because the LORD has a charge to bring against you who live in the land" (Hosea 4:1 NIV).

The southern kingdom of Judah experienced the same fate. Isaiah prophesied to them, attacking their social ills, recognizing them as symptoms of spiritual declension (Isaiah 1:3-9; 58:6-10).

They bragged about their fasting and praying, but Isaiah was quick to point out the falsity in their acts, telling them the kind of fast God wanted was for them to share their bread with the hungry, to bring to their houses the poor, to cover the nakedness of those who had nothing (Isaiah 58:7-8). "If you extend your soul to the hungry and satisfy

169

the afflicted soul, then your light shall dawn in the darkness, and your darkness shall be as the noonday. The Lord will guide you continually, and satisfy your soul in drought, and strengthen your bones. . ." (vs. 10-11 NKJ).

Isaiah unflinchingly declared "woes" on those who decreed unrighteous decrees and who robbed the needy of justice (Isaiah 10:1-2).

The prophet Micah did the same (Micah 2:1-2).

Love and concern for the poor and oppressed is central to the very nature of God.

The Psalms and Proverbs show us God's concern for the poor the hungry and the needy. To show kindness to the needy is to honor God (Proverbs 14:31).

"A generous man will himself be blessed, for he shares his food with the poor" (Prov. 22:9 NIV).

"He who gives to the poor will lack nothing, but he who closes his eyes to them receives many curses" (Prov. 28:27 NIV).

In speaking of the virtuous woman, the writer says: "She extends her hand to the poor, Yes, she reaches out her hands to the needy" (Proverbs 31:20 NKJ).

Psalm 41:1-2 speaks of the blessedness that comes to those who consider the needs of the poor; Psalm 112 contrasts the blessings of the righteous who have regard for others, and the judgment that will befall the wicked (v. 10).

Jesus' Identification with the Poor

In the New Testament, as we are introduced to God in the flesh, we stand in awe at the passages that portray the birth of Jesus. This was God incarnate in the poorest of surroundings, a cattle stall.

Following Mary's purification (according to the Levitical

Law), Joseph and Mary took their little son to Jerusalem to present Him to the Lord and to offer a sacrifice in keeping with the Law. But they were so poor they couldn't present a year-old lamb, instead they brought two turtledoves (or pigeons; see Luke 2:24; compare with Lev. 12:6-8).

The incarnation of Jesus more than anything shows us God's identification with the poor and needy. The Apostle Paul said it so well: "For you know the grace of our Lord Jesus Christ, that though He was rich, yet for your sakes He became poor, that you through His poverty might become rich" (2 Corinthians 8:9 NKJ).

Jesus didn't own a home, or have a place to call His own. "Foxes have holes and birds of the air have nests, but the Son of Man has nowhere to lay His head" (Matthew 8:20 NKJ). Think about that! Isn't that something?

His little missionary band couldn't boast any headquarters or support from a constituency. The attraction for being a part of His followers was rooted in something besides position and place. Jesus sent His disciples out with the clothes on their backs and that was it (see Luke 9:3; 10:4).

He preached to the poor (Matthew 11:5). His identification with them was complete in every way. That's why, as you look at Matthew 25 and you hear those strong words about being hungry and thirsty, you know this is real. This is actually a final judgment scene, surely one of the most magnificent passages in the Bible, a picture of how common kindness, love and concern will affect our standing in eternity. To love the less fortunate in this world, and to share from our resources, is putting our love for God into practice.

"Freely ye have received," Jesus told the disciples when He sent them out, telling them not to even take money in their belts, "freely give" (Matthew 10:8). The disciples made some sacrifices to do this. I think the question is in order for us today: What kind of commitment and what kind of sacrifices do we make?

I think of Mother Teresa, known for her compassion, acclaimed internationally for her work among the destitute and the dying, who speaks of poverty as being "joy." "Poverty is an offering that we make to God," this devout lady explains. "I don't mean that poverty consists of simply not having things. We don't become rich by having money, property or possessions. That isn't the question. What is poverty? Poverty is freedom so that what I possess doesn't hold me down, so that my possessions don't keep me from sharing or giving of myself." I believe this is what Jesus had in mind—being at His complete disposal, unhindered by the cares of this world, offering ourselves to Him wholly in devoted love.

Love like this transforms into deeds, letting Jesus live through our lives. Love, to function best, starts at home—where you live; where you work; where you worship. To radiate Christ's love around us means that the light of His love will be extended like the ripples cast by a pebble into a pond. Love with Jesus' love and the spirit of sacrifice that He demonstrated.

Mother Teresa speaks of Christ as being in "the distressing disguise of the poor." To turn our backs on the poor and hungry of this world is to turn our backs on Christ.

I first encountered the terrible plight of the poor on my around-the-world trip with Howard Carter in the great cosmopolitan city of Manchuria. We found Russians, Germans, Polish, Japanese and Chinese, besides some English-speaking people. I shall never forget what we saw. It was bitter cold; the river was frozen to a depth that large trucks were able to pass over on the ice.

People were lying along the street dead, frozen to death. Beggars had stolen their clothes, while others had kicked them to one side to let the traffic pass. We asked why they were not taken up, and were told, "Oh, soon they will be put on carts and taken outside the city and burned." Beggar women, sometimes with a child in their arms, could be seen on the street two-thirds naked, shaking with cold and dying with hunger, screaming to the passers-by for a few pennies with which to buy opium. I was a very young man in those days, but the memory of these sights and others I encountered in India and elsewhere have stayed with me.

It should be noted that the early church was mostly comprised of the poor. There might be some Christians reading this who would find it difficult to identify with those early Christians. The Apostle Paul pointed to the kind of people who were drawn into the circle of that early church: "For you see. . .that not many wise according to the flesh, not many mighty, not many noble, are called. But God has chosen the foolish things of the world to put to shame the wise, and God has chosen the weak things of the world to put to shame the things which are mighty; and the base things of the world and the things which are despised God has chosen, and the things which are not, to bring to nothing the things that are, that no flesh should glory in His presence" (1 Corinthians 1:26-29 NKJ).

What are some of those "foolish things?" In the Old Testament we find a bleeding lamb (Exodus 12), a smitten rock (Exodus 17), a brass snake (Numbers 21).

What are some of those "weak things?" A rod to defeat the Egyptians (Exodus 4), a sling to defeat a mighty giant (1 Samuel 17), a bone to defeat the Philistines (Judges 15).

What are some of those "base things"? A harlot's son who became a mighty judge (Judges 11), a heathen girl who became David's great-grandmother (Ruth 4), and an immoral woman who became a great soul-winner (John 4).

Never forget it, at both the exodus and the emergence of the early church, God chose poor folk.

As Ron Sider points out[2], one must not overstate the case. Abraham wasn't poor, Moses lived at Pharaoh's court for forty years, Luke was a doctor. Nevertheless, there is an obvious contrast between God's ways and ours. God is not impressed with wealth, size, power or status. "When God wanted to save the world, he selected slaves, prostitutes and sundry other disadvantaged folk."

If you doubt this, consider the case of just His disciples. Matthew was a Jewish tax-collector (publican) for the Roman government. No doubt this position afforded him status and money. Luke was the "beloved physician" (Colossians 4:14), and a close friend and companion of Paul. Though he was a physician by profession, he was primarily an evangelist, writing the gospel that bears his name and the book of Acts, and accompanying Paul in missionary work. But these were the only two who might have had any financial means at all. God chose these more lowly men to be His special instruments of proclaiming the good news of the gospel, and it is convincing evidence of His special concern for all those who are just ordinary people.

There is a consistent theme in the Bible that shows God's

love for the poor and downtrodden. God is not partial, but He is just. And so often, according to the biblical accounts, the rich, by lording it over the less fortunate, defraud and cheat them, they are insensitive to their problems, they oppress them, and they do not have regard for their hunger needs.

Whole nations have been destroyed because of their mistreatment of the poor. Because the Bible is so full of examples of God's compassion for the needy, how much we need to pay attention and work at getting our arteries of compassion unclogged.

That is why I am committed to calling Christians to accountability in these end-time days. And that is why we are feeding the hungry.

---

1. As cited in *The South Bend Tribune*, March 6, 1989.
2. Ronald J. Sider, *Rich Christians in an Age of Hunger* (Downers Grove, IL: Inter-Varsity Press, Second Edition 1984), p. 63.

Appendix A
How Will You Respond to the Inequities in the World?

God's people can make a difference.

Jesus left us an example. Of the thirty-six recorded miracles of Jesus during His earthly ministry, six of these were related to feeding the hungry. He wants us, His disciples today, to understand that He is vitally interested in the total person—body, soul and spirit.

In Mark 6:35-42 Jesus said to His disciples, "Give them something to eat." The people who followed Him were hungry, and He "was moved with compassion." Possibly like us, the disciples began to look at the number of people, count their money and tabulate how much it would cost. They became overwhelmed and fear paralyzed their feet.

Jesus would never have asked them to do what they could

176

not do, and because He was with them, they had eternal resources. Just so, as we respond in obedience to God's desire to see His children fed, He will miraculously bless our giving.

The Apostle Paul told the Corinthian Christians: "At the present time your plenty will supply what [others] need. . .Then there will be equality" (2 Corinthians 8:13-14 NIV).

Implications for Us Today

The Bible is clear in setting forth the responsibility of those who have toward those who have not. The implications for us, living as we are in the end times, calls for a compassionate response.

> But if any one has this world's goods—resources for sustaining life—and sees his brother and fellow believer in need, yet closes his heart of compassion against him, how can the love of God live and remain in him?
> Little children, let us not love [merely] in theory or in speech, but in deed and in truth—in practice and in sincerity"
>
> —1 John 3:17-18 (AMP)

You Can Be the Answer to Someone's Prayer

When God spoke to me in Jerusalem, He said that strong laymen were waiting for a big project to which they could joyfully give themselves without reservation, becoming a part of the end-time remnant who one day will hear His words:

> "Come, you blessed of My Father, inherit the kingdom prepared for you. . .for I was hungry and you gave me food. . ."

Then the righteous will answer Him, saying, "Lord, when did we see You hungry and feed You. . .?"

And the King will answer and say to them, "Assuredly, I say to you, inasmuch as you did it to one of the least of these My brethren, you did it to Me. . ."

—Matthew 25:34, 35a, 37a, 40 (NKJ).

The King's Court and the Queen's Court

In speaking to my heart, the Lord told me that this group of men would be called the "King's Court" and the women would be called the "Queen's Court."

We have developed parallel programs for men and women in local churches. Men and women are challenged to pray and fast, to organize rallies, and establish local fellowships.

Through your local church you can participate in specific areas of ministry that are of most concern and interest to you. Many ideas are shared with members at local meetings—things you can do individually or as a group to provide resources for The End-Time Joseph Program to Feed the Hungry.

Our primary goal is to provide for the family of God throughout the world in their times of hunger. As God's people are fed and nourished physically, they will also be ministered to in their spirits by local pastors.

In your willingness to particiapte, you will manifest the love and compassion of Christ. Because of your selfless sacrificing, we believe that you will see and experience the blessing of God in your own life.

The King's Court

Specifically, the men of the Feed-the-Hungry program

are organizing men of all nations to assist in fighting famine, building the local church into a tower of strength, and taking a harvest of lost souls from the devil. When the Lord spoke to me, He said, "The gallant men of the King's Court will contact businessmen, executives and laboring men concerning the starving people around the world. On a man-to-man basis, they will cause many men to become active in The End-Time Joseph Program."

The Queen's Court

By their God-given natures, women are uniquely endowed with tenderhearted qualities—they hurt when they see and hear about need. Their hearts are touched when they consider the plight, the tears and agony of millions of mothers weeping because they cannot feed their children. God assured me that the women's division of the Feed-the-Hungry program would be a formidable strength serving the needy in the Body of Christ around the world.

Whether you participate in a King's Court or Queen's Court through your local church or not, there are some specific things you can do alone or involved with a group. For those responding to this call of the Lord, I see the following as being essential.

Fast and Pray

We cannot feed a billion starving people without prayer. The Lord has set a challenge before us that all God's people can particiapte in through praying, fasting and giving.

We are calling for a day of fasting every Friday from sunrise to sunset, asking those who join us to contribute the value of two meals that they would miss during this fast day to Feed the Hungry.

There are several ways this can be facilitated:

1. King's Court and Queen's Court directors can encourage the formation of prayer groups in their local churches. Those involved can contribute their meal savings through their church group.

2. Those who do not belong to a local church group, but who believe in the Feed-the-Hungry program, can fast and pray and send their sacrificial gift directly to our office.

3. Those who for health reasons cannot fast, can pray and contribute the cost of two meals either through their local church or directly to our office.

Is not this the fast that I have chosen. . .Is it not to divide your bread with the hungry. . .? And if you pour out that with which you sustain your own life for the hungry, and satisfy the need of the afflicted, then shall your light rise in darkness and your obscurity and gloom be as the noonday.　　　　　　　—Isaiah 58:6a, 7a, 10 (AMP)

Be fervent in prayer.

"Arise from your bed, cry out in the night, at the beginning of the watches. Pour out your heart like water before the face of the Lord; lift up your hands toward Him for the life of your young children, who faint with hunger at the corner of every street." —Lamentations 2:19 (AMP)

Show kindness and compassion

"He who is kind to the poor lends to the Lord, and he will reward him for what he has done."—Proverbs 19:17

Be faithful.

"It is [essentially] required of stewards that a man should

be found faithful—proving himself worthy of trust."
—1 Corinthians 4:2 (AMP)

Be generous.

"For the poor will never cease from the land; therefore I command you, saying, 'You shall open your hand wide to your brother, to your poor and your needy, in your land.' "
—Deuteronomy 15:11 (NKJ)

It is time that the church recognize her God-given responsibility to come to the aid of the poor and downtrodden. The explosive message of the Old Testament is that God destroyed kingdoms because of mistreatment of the poor. If tears are the vocabulary of the anguished soul, then we who claim to be God's people must hear their cries and take upon ourselves their heartbreak and do what we can to dry those tears.

Appendix B
Major Historical Famines

c.3500 BC	Egypt	Earliest written reference to famine.
436 BC	Rome	Thousands of starving people threw themselves into the Tiber.
AD 310	England	40,000 deaths.
917-18	India Kashmir	Great mortality. Water in Jhelum River covered by bodies, "The land became densely covered with bones in all directions, until it was like one great burial-ground, causing terror to all beings."
1064-72	Egypt	Failure of Nile flood for seven years. Cannibalism.
1069	England	Norman invasion. Cannibalism.
1235	England	20,000 deaths in London; people ate bark of trees, grass.
1315-17	Central and Western Europe	Caused by excessive rain spring and summer of 1315. Deaths from starvation and disease may have been 10% over wide area.

1333-37	China	Great famine; reported 4,000,000 dead in one region only; perhaps source of Europe's Black Death.
1347-48	Italy	Famine, followed by plague (Black Death).
1557	Russia	500,000 dead. Also plague.
1630	India, Deccan	During the time of Shah Jahan, builder of the Taj Mahal, who undertook relief efforts to assist. War. Parents sold children. 30,000 reported to have died in one city, Surat. Drought followed by floods.
1650-52	Russia	Excessive rain and floods. "People ate sawdust." Many died despite tsar's permitting free grain imports. High prices prevented purchase of seed.
1677	India, Hyderabad	Great mortality. Caused by excessive rain. "All persons were destroyed by famine excepting two or three in each village."
1693	France	Awful famine—described by Voltaire.
1769	France	Five percent of population said to have died.
1769-70	India, Bengal	Caused by drought. Estimates of deaths range from 3,000,000 (a tenth of population) to 10,000,000 (a third of population).
1770	Eastern Europe	Famine and pestilence caused 168,000 deaths in Bohemia and 20,000 in Russia and Poland.
1775	Cape Verde Islands	Great famine—16,000 people died.
1790-92	India, Bombay Hyderabad, Orissa, Madras, Gujarat	The Doji Bara or skull famine, so-called because the dead were too numerous to be buried. Cannibalism.
1803-04	Western India	Caused by drought, locusts, war, and migration of starving people. Thousands died.

1837-38	Northwest India	Drought. 800,000 died.
1846-51	Ireland	Great potato famines. A million died from starvation and disease; even more emigrated.
1866	India, Bengal and Orissa	Poor distribution of rainfall. 1,500,000 deaths.
1868-70	India, Rajputana, Northwest and Central, Provinces, Punjab, Bombay.	Drought. Famine followed by fever. Deaths estimated at a fourth to a third of total population of Rajputana. In one district 90 percent of cattle died. Shortage of water for cooking and drinking.
1874-75	Asia Minor	150,000 deaths.
1876-78	India	Drought. Over 36,000,000 affected; deaths estimated at 5,000,000.
1876--79	North China	Drought for three years. Children sold. Cannibalism. Estimated deaths—9,000,000—13,000,000.
1892-94	China	Drought. Deaths estimated at 1,000,000.
1896-97	India	Drought. Widespread disease. Estimates of death range up to 5,000,000. Relief efforts successful in several areas.
1899-1900	India	Drought. Extensive relief efforts, but 1,250,000 starved. Another estimate, including effects of disease, 3,250,000.
1920-21	North China	Drought. Estimated 20,000,000 affected; 500,000 deaths
1921-22	U.S.S.R., especially Ukraine and Volga region	Drought. U.S. assistance requested by Maksim Gorky. Despite relief efforts 20,000,000-24,000,000 affected; estimates of death, 1,250,000 to 5,000,000.
1928-29	China, Shensi, Honan, and Kansu	Comparable in extent and severity to great famine of 1877-78, though because of railroads deaths, were probably less. In Shensi alone, an estimated 3,000,000 died.

1932-34	U.S.S.R.	Caused by collectivization, forced procurements, destruction of livestock by peasants. Estimated 5,000,000 died.
1941-43	Greece	War. Losses because of increased mortality and reduced births estimated at 450,000.
1941-42	Warsaw	War. Starvation, directly or indirectly, estimated to have taken 43,000 lives.
1943	Ruanda-, Urundi	35,000 to 50,000 deaths.
1943-44	India, Province of Bengal	Price of rice driven enormously high by speculation. In spite of several poor harvests, rice deficiency was small, but most people could not buy rice due to its exorbitant price. 1,500,000 died.
1947	U.S.S.R.	Reported by Khrushchev in 1963. Referring to Stalin and Molotov: "Their method was like this: they sold grain abroad, while in some regions people were swollen with hunger and even dying for lack of bread." (*Pravda,* Dec. 10, 1963.)
1960-61	Congo, Rep. of the (Kasai)	Caused by civil war. Refugees had no access to protein, resulting in epidemic of Kwashiorkor.
1965	India, Bihar	Drought. Because of tremendous success of relief operations, only thousands died, not millions.
1967-69	Nigeria, Biafra	Civil war. Government troops blockaded Biafra, a territory fighting to become independent, cutting off its food supplies. More than 1,500,000 children died from lack of protein.

1968-74	The Sahel (Sengegal, Mauritania, Mali, Upper Volta, Nigeria, Niger, and Chad)	Drought. Thirty foreign nations sent in food, but aid was extremely badly handled due to corruption of local officials, poor roads, and lack of advance planning. 500,000 people died; 5,000,000 cattle died.
1973	Ethiopia	Drought. 100,000 people died. Because Emperor Haile Selassie did not want to spoil tourist trade, he did not publicize the famine and did not ask for foreign aid.
1974	Bangladesh	Floods covered nearly half of the country, destroying stored grain and growing crops. The government did not make available to the hungry people large quantities of rice that were available, and merchants exported it to India.
1974	Somalia	Drought destroyed people and their animals. In 1975 the U.S.S.R. airlifted 120,000 starving nomads and resettled them on collective farms in the southern part of Somalia and on its coast.
1975-79	Kampuchea	1,000,000 deaths from starvation. Caused by genocidal policies of Khmer Rouge regime: massive deportations of urban population by forced march into the countryside without food or shelter; total disruption of the economic structure of the country.
1983-	Black Africa (The Sahel; eastern and southern Africa)	Prolonged drought beginning in the late 1970s; 22,000,000 people endangered in as many as 22 countries, according to UN agencies, though numbers and degree of malnourishment or starvation fluctuated. Cattle and crops afflicted as well.

Appendix C

THE WORLD HUNGER BELT

NATIONS IN WHICH HUNGER PERSISTS AS A WORLDWIDE ISSUE

This map is based on the infant mortality rate (IMR), which tells how many children per thousand die before their first birthday. Again, statistics vary, but statistics released by the World Bank in 1984 show that about 125 million children are born each year, of these some 18 million (14.5 percent) will not see their fifth birthday. And of those who die, 97 percent were born in Third World Countries.

Appendix D

THE GAP BETWEEN RICH AND POOR:

This graph, shows the gap between rich and poor nations.

☐ Developing World
■ Developed World

The Developing World Has:

75% of the World's People

15% of World Energy Consumption

17% of the World's GNP

6% of the World Health Expenditure

30% of the World's Food Grains

18% of World Export Earnings

11% of World Education Spending

8% of World Industry

5% of World Science & Technology

The Widening Gap

In 1900 the average person in the rich world had 4 times as much as a person in the poor world.

By 1970 the ratio had become 40-1

Today the pay raise that an American can expect in 1 year is greater than an Indian can expect in 100 years.

Appendix E
Scripture References

Chapter 1
Revelation 22:3; Matthew 4:13; Luke 4:14; Genesis
3:17 AMP.

Chapter 2
Genesis 12:10; 20; 26:1; 41:30, 56; Isaiah 31:1; Ruth 1:6;
2 Samuel 21:1; 1 Chronicles 21:9-13; Deuteronomy 28:53,
58; 2 Kings 6:24-29 AMP; Jeremiah 42:15-16; 44:12-29
NKJ; Lamentation 4:1-10 TLB: Ezekiel 5:16; 36:18-21; Luke
4:25, 32; 21:5-38; John 6:5-14; Mark 6:35-44; 8:1-9; 13.

Chapter 3
Revelation 6:5-8; Hosea 8:7 NAS.

Chapter 5
Matthew 2:13; Genesis 41:56-57.

Chapter 6
Matthew 2:16-18; 18:3; 19:14 NKJ; 25:34-35a, 40 NKJ;
2 Kings 6:3 AMP; Hosea 13:16; Amos 1:13; Nahum 3:10;
Genesis 16; Numbers 14:31 NKJ.

Chapter 7
Psalm 139:13-14.

Chapter 8
Matthew 26:11; John 12:3-8; Galatians 2:10; 1 Corinthians
4:14 NIV; James 2:2-17 NIV; Psalm 12; 9:18; Proverbs 19:1,
17; 28:6, 11; 29:7; Luke 16:21-31 TLB.

Chapter 9
Matthew 24:7; 1 Timothy 4:1; Romans 1:18-32; 2:9; 11:22;
Ezekiel 18:12-13;

Chapter 10
Psalm 41:1; Luke 14:12-15 NIV.

Chapter 11
Genesis 41:33-41 NKJ; 47:12.

Chapter 12
Luke 4:18; I John 3:17-18 AMP; Acts 20:35.

Chapter 13
Matthew 25:31-46; Mark 6:34, 35-42; 1 Timothy 6:17-19
NIV.

Chapter 14
Luke 16:13, 15b NIV.

190

Chapter 15

Matthew 24:42; Mark 13:8; Joel 1:15-20; 2:6; Jeremiah 4:28; Lamentations 4:8-10, 28; Revelation 6:5-6; 1 Thessalonians 5:18; Ezekiel 16:49-50 NIV; Isaiah 1:4-17; 2 Timothy 3; Daniel 4:27 NKJ.

Chapter 16

Proverbs 19:17 NIV; Exodus 3:7-8; 6:5-7; 20:2; Deuteronomy 5:6; 26:5-8; Amos 4:1; 5:10-15; Hosea 4:1, 10; Isaiah 1:3-9; 58:6-11 NKJ; 10:1-2; Micah 2:1-2; Proverbs 14:31; 22:9 NIV; 28:27 NIV; 31:20 NKJ; Psalm 41:1-2, 10; Luke 2:24; Leviticus 12:6-8; 2 Corinthians 8:9 NKJ; Matthew 8:20; Luke 9:3; 10:4; Matthew 11:5; 25; 10:8; 1 Corinthians 1:26-29 NKJ; Exodus 4; 12; 17; Numbers 21; 1 Samuel 17; Judges 11; 15; Ruth 4; John 4; Colossians 4:14.

Appendix A

Mark 6:35-42; 2 Corinthians 8:13-14 NIV; 1 John 3:17-18 AMP; Matthew 25:34-35a, 37a, 40 NKJ; Lamentations 2:19 AMP; Isaiah 58:6a, 7a, 10 AMP; Deuteronomy 15:11 NKJ; Proverbs 19:17; 1 Corinthians 4:2 AMP.

A Message to Donors and the Corporate Philanthropic Community

LeSEA Feed the Hungry is a Christian mission organization dedicated to feeding the hungry of the world.

We are desirous of making available to private donors, as well as the corporate philanthropic community, a trustworthy means of making certain their actual donations of money and/or product gets into the hands of the needy.

As a worldwide ministry, the Lester Sumrall Evangelistic Association (LeSEA) has, for over twenty years, helped people in many countries, including monetary and physical help. We are continuing direct aid programs in Poland, the Philippines, Sri Lanka, Africa, Haiti, South and Central America and other countries as the needs come to our attention.

We provide transportation and are directly involved with the actual gathering, delivery and distribution of food, clothing and relief items. This is a pastor-to-pastor program. We do not leave these items of food and necessities with local groups or national relief agencies unknown to us, but we attend to the distribution directly.

Furthermore, we are dedicated to helping the homeless and hungry in this country working through pastors and metropolitan areas where there is a concentration of desperate need.

Funds designated for a specific purpose, such as The End-Time Joseph Program to Feed the Hungry, go specifically for that project. All donations are fully tax-deductible.

Overhead expenses are kept to a minimum at LeSEA. You are welcome to tour our offices and facilities any time you are in the area.

The International Ministries of LeSEA are supported by the gifts and donations of God's people.

We believe. . .

1. The Bible to be the inspired, the only infallible, authoritative Word of God.
2. That there is one God, eternally existent in three persons: Father, Son and Holy Ghost.
3. The deity of Christ, in His virgin birth, in His sinless life, in His miracles, in His vicarious and atoning death through His shed blood, in His bodily resurrection, in His personal return in power and glory.
4. In the present ministry of the Holy Spirit, by whose indwelling the Christian is enabled to live a godly life.
5. In the resurrection of both the saved and the lost; that they are saved unto the resurrection of life and they are lost unto the resurrection of damnation.
6. In the spiritual unity of believers in Christ.

Send contributions or inquiries to:

FEED THE HUNGRY, South Bend, Indiana 46680-7777

WORLD HARVEST

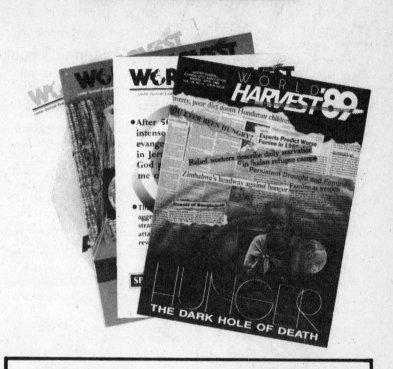

World Harvest Magazine is Dr. Sumrall's pulpit to the world. This bi-monthly magazine contains interesting articles and news about what is happening through the varied outreaches of LeSEA. Each issue also features a four-page children's section with pages to color and puzzles, etc.

For your free copy, write

World Harvest Magazine, P.O. Box 12, South Bend, Indiana, and ask to be added to the mailing list.

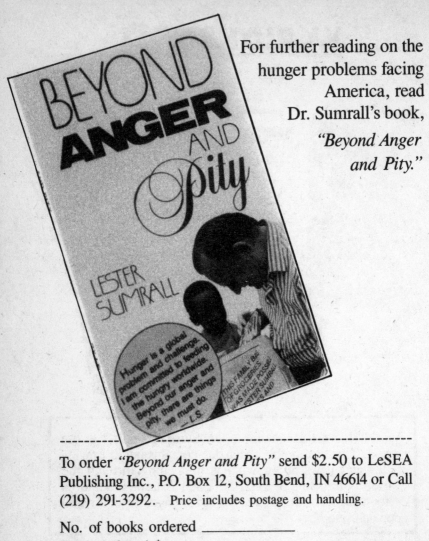

For further reading on the hunger problems facing America, read Dr. Sumrall's book, *"Beyond Anger and Pity."*

To order *"Beyond Anger and Pity"* send $2.50 to LeSEA Publishing Inc., P.O. Box 12, South Bend, IN 46614 or Call (219) 291-3292. Price includes postage and handling.

No. of books ordered _____

Total enclosed $_____

Name _____

Address _____

City, _____ State_____

Zip_____ Phone _____